KU-077-011

About this book

Symbols are used to denote the following categories:

- ⊞ map reference to maps on cover
- ✉ address or location
- ☎ telephone number
- 🕐 opening times
- ✋ admission charge
- ⅋ restaurant or café on premises or nearby
- Ⓜ nearest underground train station
- 🚌 nearest bus/tram route
- Ⓡ nearest overground train station
- ⛴ nearest ferry stop
- ✈ nearest airport
- ❓ other practical information
- ℹ tourist information office
- ➤ indicates the page where you will find a fuller description

This book is divided into five sections.

The essence of Australia pages 6–19
Introduction; Features; Food and drink;
Short break including the 10 Essentials

Planning pages 20–33
Before you go; Getting there; Getting around; Being there

Best places to see pages 34–55
The unmissable highlights of any visit to Australia

Best things to do pages 56–77
Good places to have lunch; top activities; great views; places to take the children; exceptional lesser-known destinations and more

Exploring pages 78–186
The best places to visit in Australia, organized by area

Maps
All map references are to the maps on the covers. For example, Melbourne has the reference ⊞ 21K – indicating the grid square in which it is to be found.

Admission prices
Inexpensive (under AU$10)
Moderate (AU$10–AU20)
Expensive (over AU$20)

Hotel prices
Per room per night:
$ budget (under AU$150)
$$ moderate (AU$150–AU$300)
$$$ expensive to luxury (over AU$240)

Restaurant prices
Price for a three-course meal per person without drinks:
$ budget (under AU$40)
$$ moderate (AU$40–AU$60)
$$$ expensive (over AU$60)

Contents

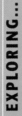

The essence of...

Visitors come to Australia for many reasons, but the continent's greatest appeal is undoubtedly its 'Great Outdoors'. The climate is generally warm and balmy, and the magnificent scenery includes rugged sandstone peaks and escarpments, rainforests, harsh Outback deserts, white-sand beaches and clear tropical waters. The unique plants, birds and animals add an exotic touch to an already dramatic landscape.

There are also many historical and cultural experiences to savour in Australia. The locals are friendly, warm and welcoming, and this relaxed atmosphere is complemented by fabulous food and wine. A visit 'Down Under' may well surprise you with its variety of experiences.

features

From white Australia's bleak convict beginnings, the country has developed into a prosperous and politically stable nation of over 20 million people. Since the early days of dependence on Britain, the national self-esteem has grown decade by decade over the past 200 or so years, and people from all over the world have settled here, making Australia today a vibrant, diverse and confident nation.

Australia – variously known as 'Down Under', 'Oz', and the 'best address on earth' – is vast: approximately 24 times the size of the British Isles and as big as continental USA (without Alaska). The terrain and climate obviously vary considerably, but overall the weather is warm and sunny, and the scenery varies from interesting to magnificent.

This benign climate has undoubtedly affected the Australian character, best described as egalitarian and relaxed. Aussies are friendly and laid-back, and visitors from everywhere are welcomed enthusiastically. This is a multicultural nation where, overall, people of European, Asian, Arabic, African Pacific Island and other origins live together in relative harmony.

Visitors should remember that Australia is enormous – it is over 4,000km (2,485 miles) from Sydney to Perth – so unless you have months to spare, select your destinations carefully.

NATURAL FEATURES

- Australia is the world's smallest and flattest continent and, after Antarctica, the driest.
- Australia's mainland coastline is a huge 36,700km (22,800 miles).
- Australia's highest point is Mount Kosciuszko in southern New South Wales – a mere 2,228m (7,310ft) high. The lowest point is 16m (52ft) below sea level at Lake Eyre in Outback South Australia.
- The Great Barrier Reef is the world's largest living, growing structure – it stretches for over 2,000km (1,240 miles) along the Queensland coast.
- The continent has over 15,000 flowering plant species, including over 700 varieties of eucalyptus.

MAKE-UP AND PEOPLE

- There are six states: New South Wales, Queensland, Victoria, Tasmania, South Australia and Western Australia; two territories: the Australian Capital Territory and the Northern Territory; and external territories, including Norfolk Island and Christmas Island.
- Although of a similar size to the United States (population over 250 million), and 24 times the size of Britain, Australia is home to only 21 million people. Around 7 million live in Sydney.
- In 2005 census the number of overseas-born Australians passed 4.8 million (24 per cent of the population), and 26 per cent of those born here had at least one overseas-born parent.

ROAD AND RAIL

- Australia has more than 810,000km (503,335 miles) of roads, but only 45 per cent are sealed.
- The world's longest straight run of railway stretches 478.4km (297 miles) from Doldea in Outback South Australia across the Nullarbor Plain in Western Australia.

food & drink

Australia's major cities are home to some world-class restaurants and a thriving café culture. Thanks to its multicultural population, authentic restaurants – from French to Vietnamese cuisines – can be found in abundance. Australia is also known for its own distinct approach to cooking, a global fusion of influences and ingredients. Dining out can be a delicious adventure or comforting home-coming.

A WORLD OF FOOD

Modern Australian (Mod-Oz) cuisine is characterized by excellent ingredients, a fusion of styles (usually East–meets–West, so perhaps a fusion of Japanese and Italian in one dish), and exquisite presentation. It's available in its purest form at top-

class restaurants, but local cafés often have their own version, with menus combining meals from a number of origins. Don't be surprised to find a laksa soup sharing menu space with foccacias and burritos.

An important component of Australia's cuisine is the superb quality and variety of local produce, from tropical fruits to Tasmania's wonderful cheeses and the freshest herbs. The quality of meat is very high, and the variety of seafood will astonish many northern hemisphere visitors: enormous prawns, oysters, crabs, lobsters and delicious wild fish such as barramundi. Australia also offers cuisines from all over the world, with Japanese, Thai and other Asian restaurants being particularly popular. You will find everything from Italian and Greek to Lebanese and African cuisines, and one of the greatest joys in this fine climate is eating al fresco, often with a marvellous sea view.

DRINKS

Wine has been produced in Australia since the late 1830s, and is among its top exports. All of the states have some involvement in the industry, and South Australia's Barossa Valley and Coonawarra region, the Hunter Valley of New South Wales, and the Margaret River area of Western Australia are some of the most famous.

Red varieties include Cabernet Sauvignon, Shiraz, Pinot Noir and Merlot, while Chardonnay, Chablis, Sauvignon Blanc and Semillon are popular whites.

There are many hundreds of different labels to choose from. Sommeliers can help to negotiate the wine list and match a wine with your meal, while wine enthusiasts might invest in James Halliday's *Australian Wine Companion* – a comprehensive guide to Australian wines.

Australian beers are known throughout the world (and Australians are known for their beer-drinking!). Pubs generally have five or six beers on tap, including a locally brewed lager and ale, as well as a few imports and perhaps a stout. Australians serve their beer cold, and with a thick creamy head. To order a beer in NSW, ask for a 'schooner' (425ml) or a 'middy' (285ml). In Victoria and Tasmania it's called a 'pot' (285ml); elsewhere just ordering a 'beer' and indicating which variety you're after will do. Pints are available almost everywhere.

As far as non-alcoholic drinks go, most Australian cities serve excellent Italian-style coffee: strong and infused through an espresso machine. Coffee fuels a café scene as vibrant as any in the world.

short break

If you only have a short time to visit Australia and would like to take home some unforgettable memories, you can do something local and capture the real flavour of the country. The following suggestions will give you a wide range of sights and experiences that won't take very long, won't cost very much and will make your visit very special. If you only have time to choose one of these, you will have found the true heart of Australia.

- **Take a cruise on Sydney Harbour** (➤ 50–51) and enjoy the beautiful scenery at the heart of the city.

- **Spend a day at the beach** to experience the sun, surf and sheer hedonism of Bondi (➤ 82) or any other of Australia's magnificent beaches. You could even have a go at surfing.

- **See a performance at the Sydney Opera House,** where you can enjoy world-class performances of theatre, music, dance and opera all under the nation's most recognizable roof (➤ 50–51).

● **Experience the Great Barrier Reef** – snorkel or dive among the colourful coral and luminous fish of this World Heritage-listed site (➤ 42–43).

● **Dine al fresco** to sample Modern Australian cuisine, especially some of the wonderful seafood, at an outdoor table with a view across the coast.

● **Visit Uluru**, at the very heart of the continent. This massive monolith is of major cultural significance to the traditional owners – the Anangu (➤ 54–55).

● **Learn about Australia's history** – discover
something of pre-European Aboriginal life at the
Australian Museum (➤ 83), or head to Port Arthur
(➤ 142) for an insight into the harsh convict days.

● **Go bushwalking** – a hike in the bush (countryside)
is a must. Explore the escarpments and eucalyptus
forests of the Blue Mountains (➤ 36–37).

● **Visit a wildlife park** for a close encounter with
kangaroos, emus, wombats, koalas and other
unique Australian animals (➤ 70–71, 87).

● **Sample local wines and beers** – spend an
evening in an Aussie pub, meet the locals, and
enjoy world-class wines and fine beers (➤ 14–15).

Planning

Before you go

WHEN TO GO

JAN	FEB	MAR	APR	MAY	JUN	JUL	AUG	SEP	OCT	NOV	DEC
26°C	26°C	25°C	22°C	19°C	17°C	16°C	18°C	20°C	22°C	24°C	25°C
79°F	79°F	77°F	72°F	66°F	63°F	61°F	65°F	68°F	72°F	75°F	77°F

🌞 🌞 ⛅ 🌧 🌧 🌦 🌦 🌦 🌦 🌦 🌤 🌞

High season   Low season

The temperatures listed above are the average daily maximum for each month in Sydney. Australia has a range of climates because of its size, geographical location and lack of high mountain ranges.

During the summer months (December to February) the southern states are the best places to visit, while Western Australia, the Northern Territory and Queensland are hot and humid.

January to March is the wet season in northern Queensland and parts of Western Australia and the Northern Territory, bringing tropical cyclones. Most of the rainfall in the Great Barrier Reef occurs in January and February. Winter (June to August) is the best time to visit the north, west and Red Centre.

WHAT YOU NEED

● Required
○ Suggested
▲ Not required

Some countries require a passport to remain valid for a minimum period (usually at least six months) beyond the date of entry; contact their consulate or embassy or your travel agent for details.

	UK	Germany	USA	Netherlands	Spain
Passport (or National Identity Card where applicable)	●	●	●	●	●
Visa (regulations can change – check before you travel)	●	●	●	●	●
Onward or Return Ticket	▲	▲	▲	▲	▲
Health Inoculations (tetanus and polio)	▲	▲	▲	▲	▲
Health Documentation (► 23, Health Insurance)	▲	▲	▲	▲	▲
Travel Insurance	○	○	○	○	○
Driving Licence (national) and International Driving Permit	●	●	●	●	●
Car Insurance Certificate (not required for rental cars)	●	●	●	●	●
Car Registration Document (not required for rental cars)	●	●	●	●	●

WEBSITES

www.australia.com
www.planbooktravel.com
www.australia.gov.au
www.immi.gov.au

www.environment.gov.au
www.bom.gov.au
www.rba.gov.au
www.aaa.asn.au

TOURIST OFFICES AT HOME

In the UK

Tourism Australia
✉ Australia Centre, Australia
House, 6th Floor, Melbourne
Place/Strand, London UK WC2B
4LG ☎ 0207 7438 4601

In the USA

Tourism Australia
✉ 6100 Center Drive
Suite 1150
Los Angeles CA 90045
☎ +310/ 229-4870

HEALTH INSURANCE

British and certain other nationals are eligible for free basic care at public hospitals but it is strongly recommended that all travellers take out a comprehensive medical insurance policy.

Dentists are plentiful and the standard of treatment is high – as are the bills. In an emergency go to the casualty wing (emergency room) of a local hospital, or locate a dentist from the local telephone book. Medical insurance is essential.

TIME DIFFERENCES

GMT	Sydney	Germany	USA (NY)	Netherlands	Spain
12 noon	10PM	1PM	7AM	1PM	1PM

Australia has three time zones. The eastern states and ACT follow Eastern Standard Time, which is 10 hours ahead of GMT (GMT+10). South Australia and the Northern Territory follow Central Standard Time (GMT+9:30) and Western Australia follows Western Standard Time (GMT+8).

Daylight Saving Time varies from state to state and is not observed in Western Australia, Queensland and the Northern Territory.

NATIONAL HOLIDAYS

1 January *New Year's Day*
26 January *Australia Day*
March/April *Good Friday*
March/April *Easter Monday*
25 April *Anzac Day*
Second Mon in June
  Queen's Birthday
  (WA: last Mon in Sep)

25 December *Christmas Day*
26 December *Boxing Day*

In addition, individual states have public holidays throughout the year for agricultural shows,

eg Brisbane Royal Show, Royal Canberra Show, Alice Springs and Hobart shows; regattas and race days, eg Melbourne Cup Day, Adelaide Cup Day and Hobart Regatta.

WHAT'S ON WHEN

As a nation, Australia spends a considerable amount of time in holiday and party mode. There are eight annual national public holidays, and each state holds at least one major festival each year. These range from the highbrow Adelaide, Melbourne and Sydney arts festivals to sporting carnivals and the bizarre Henley-on-Todd Regatta at waterless Alice Springs.

January Mid- to late Jan: *Australian Open* (tennis), Melbourne.
26 Jan: *Australia Day* holiday.
All month: *Sydney Festival* (performing arts).
February *Chinese New Year*, around Australia.
End Feb: *Gay and Lesbian Mardi Gras*, Sydney.
Tropfest (short film festival), various capital cities.
Feb/Mar: *Adelaide Festival of Arts* and *Adelaide Fringe Festival* (even-numbered years only).
Perth International Arts Festival.
Feb or Mar: *Canberra National Multicultural Festival*.
March Early Mar: *Australian Formula One Grand Prix,* Melbourne.
WOMADelaide (world music festival), Adelaide.
Royal Easter Show, Sydney.
April 25 April: *Anzac Day* holiday.

Barossa Vintage Festival (odd-numbered years only). From 1 Apr throughout the month: *Melbourne International Comedy Festival.* Easter weekend:

East Coast Roots and Blues Festival, Byron Bay.

May Early May: *Charters Towers Country Music Festival.*

June *Sydney Bienale* (contemporary art; even-numbered years). Variable: *Out of the Box Festival* for 3- to 8-year-olds (even-numbered years), Brisbane.

July Mid-Jul: *Camel Cup Carnival* (camel races), Alice Springs. *Darwin Cup Carnival* (horse races). Late July: *Royal Darwin Show.* *Brisbane Festival* (performing arts, even-numbered years).

August Late Aug: *Melbourne Writers Festival.* Aug to Sep: *Festival of Darwin.* Late Aug: *Alice Springs Rodeo.*

September Late Sep: *AFL Grand Final* (Australian Rules football), Melbourne. Mid-Sep to mid-Oct: *Floriade Spring Festival,* Canberra. *Henley-on-Todd Regatta,* Alice Springs. *Festival Cairns* (performing arts).

October Mid-Oct: *Gold Coast Indy Carnival* (motor race). *Manly International Jazz Festival,* Sydney. *Melbourne International Arts Festival.*

November First Tue: *Melbourne Cup* (horse race). Late Nov: *Fremantle Festival.*

December Late Dec: *Hobart Summer Festival.*

Getting there

BY AIR

Sydney Airport

� 13 minutes

🚌 35 minutes

🚗 25 minutes

8km (5 miles) to city centre

Darwin Airport

🚁 N/A

🚌 15 minutes

🚗 15 minutes

13km (8 miles) to city centre

All major airlines operate services to Australia. Qantas, the Australian national airline, flies from London to Australia's international airports. Flights from Europe take between 20 and 30 hours; flights from North America take about 15 hours. Many other international carriers such as British Airways, Singapore Air, Malaysia Airlines and Cathay Pacific fly to state capitals, with Melbourne and Sydney being the busiest.

NEW SOUTH WALES Sydney Airport (www.sydneyairport.com.au) The Sydney Airporter (www.kst.com.au/airport.php) bus runs every 15 minutes and operates a door-to-door service from the airport to a variety of accommodation in the city, around Darling Harbour and Kings Cross (bookings required). A fast train service – the Airport Link (www.airportlink.com.au) – runs straight into Central Station every 10–15 minutes during peak times.

VICTORIA Melbourne Airport (www.melair.com.au) is 25km (15 miles) away, and can be reached by taxi or shuttlebus. Taxis are expensive and take 30 minutes, whereas the Skybus (www.skybus.com.au) is less expensive and operates a 24-hour service between Melbourne airport and Southern Cross Station downtown (20 minutes). Buses depart from the airport every 15 minutes between 6am and 9:30pm and half-hourly or hourly at other times.

Skybus also operates a free minibus shuttle service between Southern Cross Station and hotels in the Central Business District (CBD).

QUEENSLAND Brisbane Airport (www.bne.com.au) is 13km (8 miles) from the city, which can be reached by taxi, train and bus.

Taxis are direct but expensive and can be found outside all terminals. The Airtrain (www.airtrain.com.au) takes 20 minutes to the CBD and runs every 15 minutes from outside the terminals at the domestic and international airports. Trains stop at Bowen Hills, Brunswick Street, Central, Roma Street, South Brisbane and Southbank and run half-hourly to the Gold Coast.The cheapest transfer option is to take the Coachtrans (www.coachtrans.com.au) shuttle bus, which runs to the city every 30 minutes from 5:45am to 1:15pm. Coachtrans also runs frequent transfers to the Gold Coast.

Also in Queensland, **Cairns Airport** (www.cairnsairport.com.au) is 7km (5 miles) outside the town and can easily be reached by taxi. Sun Palm's (www.sunpalmtransport.com) airport shuttle bus service operates inexpensive transfers between the airport and most hotels, as well as to Port Douglas and Cape Tribulation.

NORTHERN TERRITORY Darwin Airport (www.darwin-airport.com.au) is easily reached by taxi (around $30) or the Airport Shuttle ($10) which transfers from the airport to hotel accommodation.

SOUTH AUSTRALIA Adelaide Airport (www.aal.com.au) is only 7km (4 miles) from the city and has good links to Adelaide by taxi or by Skylink (www.skylinkadelaide.com), a shuttle service running every half-hour and hour to hour daily.

WESTERN AUSTRALIA Perth Airport (www.perthairport.net.au) is 10km (6 miles) from the city, reached by taxi (around $40) or the Perth Airport Shuttle bus ($15, www.perthshuttle.com.au). This runs to Perth city and Fremantle, stopping at most central accommodation areas.

BY SEA
Many world cruises dock at major port cities in Australia as part of their itinerary. An informative website on sea travel is www.cruisecritic.com

Getting around

PUBLIC TRANSPORT

Internal flights Australia has a wide network of domestic and regional air services, and air travel between states is often the best form of transport. Qantas (www.qantas.com.au), Jetstar (www.jetstar.com.au), Virgin Blue (www.virginblue.com. au) and Tiger Airways (www.tigerairways.com) are the main domestic airlines, and often offer discount deals on accommodation and car rental as well as flights.

Trains Most capital cities have frequent train services between business districts and the suburbs. Long-distance trains offer sleeping berths and reclining seats, and most interstate trains have dining or buffet cars. If you are booking ahead from outside Australia, enquiries and reservations are handled by Rail Australia (www.railaustralia.com.au).

Bus travel Excellent long-distance express bus services run daily between major cities, serviced by Greyhound (tel: 1300 473 946, www.greyhound.com.au). Coaches are non-smoking, have air-conditioning and bathrooms. Tasmania is serviced by Tasmanian Redline Coaches (tel: 1300 360 000; www.redlinecoaches.com.au) and Tassie Link (tel: 1300 300 520; www.tigerline.com.au).

Ferries The only regular interstate ferry service is the Spirit of Tasmania passenger/vehicle ferry between Melbourne and Devonport in Tasmania (daily service; twice daily during summer). For more information, tel: 1800 634 906; www.spiritoftasmania.com.au

Urban transport Most state capital cities have good train services and/or frequent bus services that operate between the city centre and the suburbs. Perth, Brisbane and Sydney also have regular local ferry services. Trams or light railways run in Melbourne, Adelaide and Sydney.

For transport information in Sydney: tel: 131500; www.131500.com.au
Melbourne: tel: 13 16 38; www.metlinkmelbourne.com.au
Perth: tel: 13 62 13; www.transperth.wa.gov.au

Brisbane: tel: 13 12 30;
www.translink.com.au
Adelaide: ☎ (08) 8218 2362;
www.transadelaide.com.au
Taxis All taxis in Australia display
the fare on a meter. Taxis can be
booked or stopped on the street.

DRIVING

- Drive on the left.
- Speed limit on motorways: 100–110kph (62–68mph)
  Speed limit on urban roads: 40–60kph (25–37mph)
  Obey the speed limits. There are speed cameras throughout the
  country and hefty speeding fines.
- It is compulsory to wear seat belts at all times.
- Random breath-testing. Never drive under the influence of alcohol.
- Filling stations are plentiful, except in some Outback areas, but
  business hours may vary. Most service stations accept international
  credit cards.

CAR RENTAL

Rental cars are available at major air and rail terminals and from cities
throughout Australia. It is advisable to book ahead, especially during
December and January. Most rental companies offer advice and provide
relevant guides and maps.

If your rental car breaks down you should contact the rental company,
which will arrange to send road service to your location and repair the
vehicle. Alternatively, most service stations will be able to assist or, at
least, direct you to the nearest repair centre.

FARES AND TICKETS

Long-distance train and bus tickets and domestic airline tickets can be
bought online, at stations and airports and from some travel agents.
In cities, public transport tickets can be bought on-board or at departure
points. There are few travel discounts for foreign visitors.

Museums and galleries normally offer the concession (discount) entry
price for holders of an International Student Identity Card (ISIC).

Being there

TOURIST OFFICES
● Canberra Visitor Centre (ACT)
✉ 330 Northbourne Avenue,
Dickson ☎ (02) 6205 0044
www.canberratourism.com.au
● Sydney Visitor Centre (NSW)
✉ Corner of Argyle and Playfair
streets, The Rocks ☎ (02) 9240
8788; www.visitnsw.com
● Brisbane Visitor Centre
✉ Queen Street Mall ☎ (07) 3006
6200; www.queenslandholidays.
com.au
● Western Australia Visitor Centre
✉ Corner of Forrest Place and
Wellington Street, Perth
☎ (08) 9483 1111;

www.westernaustralia.com
● Tourism NT
✉ Tourism House, 43 Mitchell
Street, Darwin ☎ (08) 8999 3900;
www.tourismnt.com
● South Australia Visitor and Travel
Centre ✉ 18 King William Street,
Adelaide ☎ (08) 8303 2220;
www.southaustralia.com
● Melbourne Visitor Information
Centre ✉ Federation Square,
Melbourne ☎ (03) 9658 9658;
www.visitvictoria.com.au
● Tasmanian Travel and Information
Centre ✉ 20 Davey Street, Hobart
☎ (03) 6230 8233
www.discovertasmania.com

MONEY
The monetary unit of Australia is the Australian dollar (AU$) and the cent
(100¢ = AU$1). Coins come in 5¢, 10¢, 20¢, 50¢ and $1 and $2
denominations, and there are $5, $10, $20, $50 and $100 notes. Major
credit cards are accepted in all large cities and most airports and banks
have facilities for changing foreign currency and traveller's cheques.

TIPS/GRATUITIES

Yes ✓   No ✗

Restaurants (if service not included)	✓	10%
Cafés/bars	✓	10%
Taxis	✓	round-up the fare
Porters	✓	$1–$2/bag
Chambermaids	✗	
Cloakroom attendants	✗	
Toilets	✗	

POSTAL AND INTERNET SERVICES

Post offices (www.auspost.com.au) are found across the country; combined with a general store in smaller places. Postal and poste restante (mail pickup) services are available. Mail boxes are red with a white 'P'. Internet cafés abound in Australian cities and an increasing number of hotels and cafes offer Wi-Fi access.

TELEPHONES

Long-distance calls within Australia (STD) and International Direct Dialling (IDD) can be made on public payphones which accept coins and phonecards, available from newsagents and milkbars in denominations of AU$5, $10 and $20. The International Direct service gives access to over 50 countries for collect or credit-card calls. A Telstra PhoneAway prepaid card enables you to use virtually any phone in Australia with all call costs charged to the card.

Emergency telephone numbers
Police, Fire and Ambulance: 000

International dialling codes
To call from Australia to:
UK: 0011 44
Germany: 0011 49

USA/Canada: 0011 1
Netherlands: 0011 31
Spain: 0011 34

EMBASSIES AND CONSULATES

UK ☎ (02) 6270 6666; Canberra
Germany ☎ (02) 6270 1911; Canberra
USA ☎ (02) 6214 5600; Canberra

Netherlands ☎ (02) 6220 9400; Canberra
Spain ☎ (02) 6273 3555; Canberra

ELECTRICITY

The power supply is 220/240 volts, 50 cycles AC.

Sockets accept three-flat-pin plugs so you may need an adaptor. If your appliances are 110v check if there is a 110/240v switch; if not you will need a voltage converter. Universal outlets for 240v or 110v shavers are usually found in leading hotels.

PLANNING

HEALTH AND SAFETY

Sun advice The sun in Australia is extremely strong, especially in summer. Cover up skin, avoid sunbathing in the middle of the day. Use a high-SPF sunscreen.

Drugs Prescription and non-prescription drugs are available from pharmacies. Visitors may import up to three months' supply of prescribed medication: bring a doctor's certificate.

Safe water It is safe to drink tap water throughout Australia.

Personal safety The usual safety precautions should be taken.

- Hitchhiking is not recommended and is strongly discouraged by the Australian government.
- Avoid walking alone in unpopulated areas at night.
- If bushwalking or camping, leave an itinerary with friends. Wear boots, socks and trousers. Carry water with you.
- Take care and heed warning signs when swimming, whether in the sea or fresh water (crocodiles!).
- Avoid swimming at beaches in the northern parts of Australia during the wet season (from around Oct–Apr), due to deadly stingers.
- Surf only on patrolled beaches and swim between the flags.

OPENING HOURS

- Shops
- Banks
- Post Offices
- Museums/Monuments
- Pharmacies

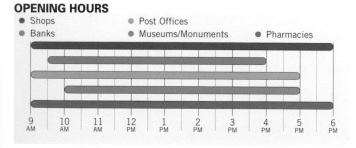

Shops: Hours vary from state to state. Many supermarkets and department stores stay open until 9pm on Thu and/or Fri. Some supermarkets in larger cities are open daily until midnight. Banks: Open Mon–Fri 9–5. Some open Saturday morning. Museums: Hours may vary. Pharmacies: Some are open longer hours, including 24-hour services in larger cities.

LANGUAGE

The common language of Australia is English, but it has been adapted and modified to form 'Strine', a colourful and abbreviated version of the mother tongue. The rather nasal Australian accent is quite distinctive and is spoken without any real regional variation throughout the country. The vocabulary contains a number of words of Aboriginal origin (didgeridoo and kangaroo), but the real joy of 'Strine' is its slang. The following is a short list of words and abbreviations you may encounter.

arvo	afternoon	*interstate*	anything to do with the other Australian states
barbie	barbecue		
bludger	scrounger		
blue	a fight, or a redhead	*jackaroo*	young male trainee on a station (farm)
bottle shop	off-licence/liquor store		
bush	countryside	*joey*	baby kangaroo
bushranger	outlaw	*lollies*	sweets, candy
BYO	bring your own (drink to a restaurant)	*lamington*	a square of sponge cake covered in chocolate icing and coconut
cask	wine-box		
chook	chicken	*ripper*	good (also 'little ripper')
chunder	to vomit		
cockie	farmer	*sandshoes*	trainers, sneakers
crook	ill	*semi-trailer*	articulated truck
dead set	correct, spot on	*shoot through*	to leave
dinkum	genuine	*snags*	sausages
drongo	slow-witted person	*sprog*	baby
dunny	outside lavatory	*station*	large farm or ranch
esky	large insulated box for keeping beer or refreshments cold	*strides*	trousers
		stubby	small bottle of beer
		Tassie	Tasmania
fossicking	hunting for precious stones	*tinny*	can of beer
		unit	apartment, flat
galah	a kind of parrot, an idiot	*ute*	utility truck (pickup truck)
garbo	garbage collector	*wowser*	prude, killjoy
g'day	good day, traditional Australian greeting	*yakka*	work

Best places to see

1 Blue Mountains, New South Wales

www.bluemts.com.au

For a complete change to Sydney's waterfront glamour, visit these nearby mountains to experience the great natural beauty of their geological wonders.

This is one of Australia's most popular holiday destinations. Visitors come to the Blue Mountains to experience their wild grandeur, mist-filled valleys, rich Aboriginal and European heritage, and to escape the summer heat. The cold winters allow visitors to enjoy the charm of open fires. Just two hours by road or train from Sydney, the mountains get their name from their blue haze.

There is so much to do and see here, from just taking in the panoramic views from the many escarpment lookouts to walking in the temperate rainforests which line the ravines and valleys. Waterfalls cascade off the cliffs into valleys far below, where they join streams that disappear

into dense vegetation. The golden brown of ancient, weathered rock faces, formed by the action of the elements over millions of years, contrasts with the distinctive blue-green of the mountain vegetation.

Because of the great range and diversity of land forms and plant communities, and its habitats sheltering rare or endangered fauna, the Greater Blue Mountains region became a World Heritage Site in 2000. In addition to its natural sights and adventure sports, there are myriad galleries, antiques shops, gardens, museums and fine eating establishments to enjoy. From the mountain town of Katoomba, explore the unique surrounds from the steep Scenic Railway, Cableway or Skyway (with a glass-bottom floor). The stunning Jenolan Caves' limestone formations are nearby.

🚼 23J 🚃 From Sydney; stops at various mountain towns. Driving is another option
🅿 A wide range of accommodation from B&Bs to five star. Many tour companies operate day tours from Sydney
🛈 Information centres ✉ Great Western Highway, Glenbrook; ✉ Echo Point, Katoomba ☎ 1300 653 408 or 1800 641 227
🅦 Glenbrook: daily 9–5. Closed 25 Dec

2 Cairns and District, North Queensland

www.tropicalaustralia.com.au

Cairns is the perfect base for a superb nature-based holiday allowing trips to the World Heritage-listed reefs and rainforests as well as the dry Outback.

With its international airport, well-developed tourism infrastructure and proximity to natural attractions such as the Great Barrier Reef, tropical rainforests and Atherton Tableland, Cairns is the 'tourist capital' of North Queensland. Here are dozens of hotels, restaurants and shops, and many options for cruises – as well as diving, fishing or

snorkelling trips – to the reef. Excellent beaches stretch to the north of town, and adventure activities like whitewater rafting and bungee jumping are popular. Around town you can visit the Cairns Museum and the Pier Marketplace, or just soak up the city's relaxed, tropical atmosphere. North of the city is the pretty coastal town of Port Douglas, while further afield are Mossman and the Daintree rainforests.

Inland from Cairns, the cool upland region of the Atherton Tableland, with its fertile farming land, volcanic lakes, waterfalls and rainforest, presents a striking contrast to the hot, humid coast. Kuranda (27km/17 miles away) offers colourful markets, a tourist park with wildlife section and river cruises. You can reach Kuranda by road, on the spectacular Skyrail Rainforest Cableway, or by travelling on the famous Kuranda Scenic Railway, which winds its way up the Great Dividing Range.

For a complete change, take a trip inland to the Gulf Savannah country and sample the hospitality of the Outback locals. Discover the grasslands, wetlands, escarpments and the Undara Volcanic National Park.

✚ 10C 🖐 Inexpensive–expensive ✖ Cairns
❓ Huge variety of accommodation from backpacker to five star. Car rental agencies are numerous, and there are many bus services and tours to all popular destinations
ℹ️ Tourism Tropical North Queensland ✉ 51 The Esplanade, Cairns ☎ (07) 4051 3588
ℹ️ Port Douglas Tourist Information Centre ✉ 23 Macrossan Street, Port Douglas ☎ (07) 4099 5599
ℹ️ Kuranda Visitor Information Centre ☎ (07) 40939311

3 Gold Coast, Queensland

www.goldcoasttourism.com.au

Although not to everyone's liking, the brash and sometimes crass Gold Coast reveals a very different side of Australia from its natural wonders.

It would be difficult not to have a good time on this lively, highly developed 70km (43-mile) strip of coastline to the south of Brisbane. Stretching down to Coolangatta on the New South Wales border, the Gold Coast offers consistently warm temperatures and an average of 300 days of sunshine each year. The sandy beaches are lapped by clear blue waters that are perfect for swimming, surfing and all kinds of water sports, and there is a smorgasbord of man-made attractions and entertainment.

The heart of the action is the appropriately named Surfers Paradise, the main town, which offers excellent shopping and dining and a host of nightlife options, including the glossy Jupiters

Casino at nearby Broadbeach. Many of the Gold Coast's attractions are particularly appealing to children, and theme parks like Dreamworld, Warner Bros Movie World, Wet 'n' Wild Water World and the excellent Sea World are extremely popular. There are many fine golf courses in the area and you can take a cruise to tranquil South Stradbroke Island, go waterskiing, or even sample the daredevil sport of bungee jumping. The Coast's list of things to do is almost endless.

If you prefer to stay somewhere quieter, the southern area around Coolangatta and Tweed Heads offers a less frenetic pace – and fewer high-rise buildings. When you've had enough of the coast, a short trip to the hinterland, particularly to Lamington National Park (➤ 113) or the delightful mountain town of Mount Tamborine, is a rewarding experience. Excellent scenery and a cooler environment, with rainforest walking trails and a diversity of art and craft shops, make this town a great day trip.

➕ 24H 🚌 Coach transfers (from Brisbane) 🚆 Gold Coast (from Brisbane) ✈ Coolangatta
ℹ Gold Coast Tourism Bureau ✉ 2 Cavill Avenue, Surfers Paradise ☎ (07) 5538 4419 🕐 Mon–Fri 8:30–5:30, Sat 8:30–5, Sun 9–4

4 Great Barrier Reef, Queensland

www.gbrmpa.gov.au
www.queenslandholidays.com

The Great Barrier Reef is often described as the eighth wonder of the world, and a visit to this marine wonderland will be long remembered.

Running parallel to the Queensland coast for over 2,000km (1,240 miles) – from Papua New Guinea to just south of the Tropic of Capricorn – the Great Barrier Reef is the world's largest living structure. This extraordinary ecosystem is, in fact, made of over 2,000 linked reefs and around 700 islands and fringing reefs, and is composed of and built by countless tiny coral polyps and algae. This famous natural attraction is protected by its Great Barrier Reef Marine Park status and World Heritage listing.

The reef itself is home to many different types of coral: some are brightly coloured, while others, like the aptly named staghorns, take on strange formations. The reef's tropical waters host an incredible variety of marine life – everything from tiny, luminously coloured fish to sharks, manta rays, turtles and dolphins. There are many ways to view and explore this fabulous underwater world: scenic

flights, boat trips, snorkelling or scuba-diving, and glass-bottom or semi-submersible boat trips are all available.

For the very best Great Barrier Reef experience, it is possible to stay right on the reef. The idyllic coral cays of Green Island, Heron Island and Lady Elliot Island offer resort accommodation, while Lady Musgrave is for campers only. Other options are to base yourself at a coastal resort (Townsville, Cairns and Port Douglas in the north, or the Whitsunday Islands further south are the best bets) or on one of the many non-reef islands. Some island suggestions are Lizard, Dunk and Magnetic islands in the north; Hayman, South Molle and Hamilton in the Whitsunday region; and Great Keppel Island in the south.

✚ 11C 🚌 or ✈ Proserpine, Townsville, Cairns

5 Great Ocean Road, Victoria

www.greatoceanrd.org.au

A journey along Australia's most spectacular road reveals superb coastal scenery, charming seaside resorts and fishing villages, and a forested hinterland.

Extending from Torquay to Warnambool, Victoria's Great Ocean Road (GOR) snakes its way along the state's southwest coast for 300km (185 miles). Geelong, 75km (46 miles) from Melbourne, is the state's second-largest city and a 30-minute drive from the start of the GOR. Torquay, and nearby Bells Beach, are popular with surfers. The quiet village of Anglesea is famous for the kangaroos that roam its local golf course, while Lorne offers fine beaches, a delightful seaside resort atmosphere and access to the magnificent Great Otway National Park. Covering over 100,000ha (247,100 acres), it protects stunning waterfalls and rainforest walks.

The coast is most dramatic as you reach Port Campbell National Park. The spectacular formations here known as the Twelve Apostles are the result of erosion caused by wind, rain and the stormy Southern Ocean. The picturesque town of Port Campbell is an ideal base for exploring.

Further west along this wild coastline, the aptly named Shipwreck Coast is famous for migrating whales, which give birth here between June and September each year. The Great Ocean Road proper ends at the regional centre of Warnambool. Just beyond is the historic fishing village of Port Fairy, with many original bluestone buildings, beaches and coastal cruises.

🚻 21L 🚌 V line: Apollo Bay to Warrnambool, Fri only; driving is the best option 🚉 From Geelong to Warrnambool ❓ Great Ocean Walk: from Apollo Bay to the Twelve Apostles; www.greatoceanwalk.com.au 🛈 Geelong and Great Ocean Road Visitor Centre ✉ Princes Highway, Geelong ☎ 1800 620 888 or (03) 5275 5797 🕐 Daily 9–5

6 Kakadu National Park, Northern Territory

www.deh.gov.au/parks/kakadu
http: en.travelnt.com

Australia's largest national park is both a superb tropical wilderness and a treasure house of ancient Aboriginal art and culture.

Covering almost 20,000sq km (7,720sq miles) three hours from Darwin, this vast World Heritage-listed national park is one of Australia's most spectacular attractions. Much of Kakadu is a flat, river-crossed floodplain that transforms into a lake during the wet season, but this large area is backed by forested lowlands, hills and the dramatic 250m (820ft) cliffs of the Arnhem Land escarpment. The extraordinary wildlife within this varied terrain ranges from giant saltwater crocodiles to dingoes, wallabies, snakes, goannas and over 280 species of birds.

There is much evidence of the area's long Aboriginal occupation, which may have endured for an incredible 50,000 years. Aboriginal-owned Kakadu includes Nourlangie and Ubirr rocks, where you can see fine examples of Aboriginal rock art, estimated to be around 20,000 years old. Among the park's scenic highlights are the spectacular Jim Jim Falls and Twin Falls that tumble off the escarpment, and Yellow Water – a tranquil waterhole and wetlands area, home to prolific birdlife.

During the wet season (October to March) many of the roads are impassable, so the best time to visit Kakadu is during the 'Dry' (April to September). Much of the park can be explored in a conventional vehicle, but a four-wheel drive is necessary for some unsealed roads. Comprehensive information is available from Bowali Visitor Centre, and the Warradjan Aboriginal Cultural Centre at Yellow Water provides further insights into the area's indigenous culture and history.

From Kakadu, you can cross the croc-infested East Alligator River into the vast Aboriginal Reserve of Arnhem Land. Join a tour to visit Gunbalanya (Oenpelli) – a small Aboriginal township and its arts centre.

➕ 7B 👣 Moderate 🍴 Cafés in Jabiru and at resorts ($–$$) ✈ Darwin ❓ Guided walks from visitor centre 🛈 Bowali Visitor Centre ✉ Kakadu Highway ☎ (08) 8938 1121 🕐 Daily 8–5

7

The Kimberley, Western Australia

www.kimberleytourism.com

In the far north of Western Australia, the Kimberley is one of the continent's remotest and most spectacular regions.

Explored and settled as late as the 1880s, the Kimberley is extremely rugged and very sparsely settled – the population of around 35,000 lives in Aboriginal settlements, on enormous cattle stations, and in a few small towns. This vast region of 420,000sq km (162,120sq miles) is generally divided into two main areas, the West and East Kimberley.

The tropical town of Broome, with its multicultural population, pearling history and fabulous beaches, is the ideal starting point for exploring the western region. From the nearby settlement of Derby, join a tour to witness the

massive 9m (29ft) tides surge through a narrow passage between cliffs to form the 'Horizontal Waterfall'.

You can reach the East Kimberley by driving northeast from Broome or flying to Kununurra, a town near the Northern Territory border and the base for the ambitious 1960s and 1970s Ord River Irrigation Scheme. This project created the vast Argyle and Kununurra lakes – welcome breaks in the otherwise arid landscape. From here you can visit the remote and wondrous Bungle Bungles. Contained within Purnululu National Park, 'discovered' only in 1983, and given World Heritage status in 2003, these spectacular rock formations, up to 300m (985ft) high, are composed of extremely crumbly silica and sandstone eroded into beehive-like shapes.

Other attractions worth seeing in this wild, last-frontier landscape include Mirima National Park near Kununurra, often referred to as 'the mini Bungle Bungles', Windjana Gorge National Park, known for its freshwater crocodile population, and the amazing Wolfe Creek Crater – the enormous depression left when a 50,000-tonne meteorite crashed here 300,000 years ago.

✚ 5C ✖ Broome or Kununurra ❓ Best visited Apr–Oct. Rental of a four-wheel-drive vehicle is recommended. Purnululu National Park closed Jan–Mar

ℹ West Kimberley Tourist Bureau ✉ Corner of Broome Road and Short Street, Broome; East Kimberley Tourist Bureau ✉ Coolibah Drive, Kununurra; Broome Visitor Centre ☎ (08) 9192 2222; Kununurra Visitor Centre ☎ (08) 9168 1177 🕐 Daily, generally 9–4

8 Sydney Harbour and Sydney Opera House

www.sydneyoperahouse.com

Complemented by the ethereal, sail-like outlines of the famous Opera House, Sydney Harbour is the glittering jewel of Australia's most famous city.

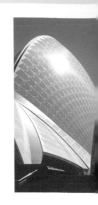

From the day in January 1788 when the 11 convict-bearing ships of the First Fleet sailed into Port Jackson, Sydney's harbour has been the focus of this great city. A harbour cruise – be it on a luxury boat or a humble Sydney ferry – is a must. From the

water you will see the city, including the large areas of the Sydney Harbour National Park, from a unique perspective. Ferries are also the best way to reach waterfront suburbs and the harbour's beaches. From Circular Quay you can take a trip to the beaches of Manly on the north side of the harbour, or to the southside suburb of Watsons Bay, close to the harbour's entrance. Ferries also visit some of the national park's islands, including historic Fort Denison.

On the harbour's southern shore, the curved roofs of the Sydney Opera House soar above Bennelong Point. Completed in 1973, after 14 years in the making and many technical and political problems, this architectural masterpiece, designed by Danish architect Jorn Utzon, gained immediate iconic status. The structure's stone platform and dramatic white roofs, covered with over a million ceramic tiles, have made it one of the world's most distinctive buildings – World Heritage listed in 2007. Once you have inspected the exterior, attending a performance or taking a guided tour of one of the six performance venues is highly recommended.

Above the magnificent harbour is the third ingredient of this classic Sydney scene: the Sydney Harbour Bridge (► 85), completed in 1932 and, with a tunnel running underground, still the major link between the south and north shores.

🔲 *Sydney 4a* ✉ Opera House: Bennelong Point
☎ Performance details (02) 9250 7777; tours: (02) 9250 7250;
www.sydneyoperahouse.com 🎟 Moderate–expensive
🍴 Guillaume at Bennelong restaurant ($$$), cafés ($–$$)
🚇 Circular Quay ❓ Guided tours 9 and 5. Performances include opera, ballet, classical music and theatre

9 Tasmania's World Heritage Area

www.parks.tas.gov.au

Much of Tasmania is superb wilderness, and the island's relatively small size makes these untouched areas easily accessible.

Tasmania's wilderness is of such significant natural beauty that around 20 per cent – an incredible 1.38 million ha (3.4 million acres) – of the state is under World Heritage protection. Made up of a number of national parks, it includes rugged peaks, wild rivers, moorland and remote coastline, as well as historic sites. Wildlife includes Tasmanian devils, echidnas and the elusive platypus.

One of the most accessible regions in the World Heritage Area is the Cradle Mountain–Lake St Clair National Park, just 170km (105 miles) from the capital, Hobart. The alpine scenery here is truly spectacular – including high peaks such as Mount Ossa (1,617m/5,305ft) – the state's highest mountain lakes, alpine moorlands and rainforests. There are many hiking trails here, the most famous of which is the 65km (40-mile) Overland Track in the heart of the Cradle Mountain– Lake St Clair National Park.

To the south, the Franklin-Gordon Wild Rivers National Park is particularly famous for its adventurous Franklin River whitewater rafting.

Even more remote and untamed wilderness is found in the Southwest National Park, the domain of forests, lakes and a long, deeply indented coastline. Experienced hikers will enjoy the challenge of this park's 85km (53-mile) South Coast Track. Much closer to Hobart and characterized by its heathlands and rugged dolerite ranges is the Hartz Mountains National Park.

November to April are the best months to explore these areas, but the weather can be unpredictable at any time, changing in minutes from warm and sunny to rain, or even snow.

✚ 22L and 22M 🖐 Parks: inexpensive 🚌 From Hobart, Devonport and Launceston to some locations; driving is the best option ❓ www.overlandtrack.com.au for bookings ℹ️ Tasmanian Parks and Hobart Wildlife Service ✉️ 134 Macquarie Street, Hobart ☎ 1300 135 513 or (03) 6233 6191 🕐 Mon–Fri 9–5

10 Uluṟu-Kata Tjuṯa National Park, Northern Territory

www.deh.gov.au/parks/uluru/
www.centralaustraliantourism.com

This 1,325ha (3,275-acre) World Heritage Site incorporates two of Australia's most spectacular sights – Uluṟu (Ayers Rock) and neighbouring Kata Tjuṯa (The Olgas).

Located at the centre of the continent, Uluṟu's vast bulk is an extraordinary and overwhelming sight. At 348m (1,142ft) high and with a base circumference of some 9km (5.5 miles), this is one of the world's largest monoliths – a massive rock which is made even more dramatic by its setting on the vast open plains of the Red Centre. Uluṟu was first sighted by Europeans in 1872, but this area has been sacred to the local Anangu people for tens of thousands of years. It is possible to climb Uluṟu, but the activity is discouraged by the Anangu landowners as the rock is a sacred site; under traditional law, climbing is prohibited to everyone except senior men initiated into Anangu culture. The climb can also be dangerous; people have died attempting to ascend the monolith and many have been injured. The best option is to hike around the base, and to view Uluṟu at sunset, when its normally dark red colour changes dramatically as the light fades.

Although, like Uluṟu, it is the tip of a vast underground formation, Kata Tjuṯa, 30km (18 miles) to the west, offers a rather different experience.

The name means 'many heads' – an appropriate description of the 30 or so massive rocks which make up Kata Tjuṯa. The domes are sacred and are strictly off limits to visitors. Access is permitted on the two established walking trails: the Nalpa Gorge walk (2.6km/1.6 miles; 1 hour) and the Valley of the Winds (7.4km/4.6 miles, 3 hours).

A visit to the Uluṟu-Kata Tjuṯa Cultural Centre, just 1km (0.5 miles) from Uluṟu, is a must. This excellent complex includes displays on Aboriginal culture and history, films of traditional art and dance, and a shop that sells local arts and crafts. The base for exploring the national park is the well-designed Ayers Rock Resort village of Yulara.

✚ 6E 🕐 Dec–Feb daily 5am–9pm; Mar 5:30am–8:30pm; Apr 6am–8pm; May 6am–7:30pm; Jun–Jul 6:30am–7:30pm; Aug 6am–7:30pm; Sep 5:30am–7:30pm; Oct–Nov 5am–8pm (parts of the park may be temporarily closed for cultural reasons and due to weather conditions) ✈ Connellan airport 🛈 Cultural centre ☎ (08) 8956 1128 🕐 Daily 7–6 ✋ Expensive

Best things to do

Best wildlife encounters

Australia's unique wildlife can also be elusive, either being nocturnal or well disguised in its natural surrounds. Sanctuaries and wildlife parks guarantee more wildlife sightings than years of watching in the wild could, and the displays generally resemble the creature's natural environment. But nothing beats seeing a 5m (16-foot) saltwater croc cruising on a river (from the safety of the riverbank, of course), or swimming in the sea with giant manta rays. Following are some of the country's, and nature's, best wildlife encounters.

The Great Barrier Reef, Queensland, ➤ 42–43
Come face to face with a giant grouper as you both swim around colourful coral. And it's just one of the 1,500 fish species found at the Great Barrier Reef, which you can experience by diving, snorkelling or boating. Keep a look out for sea horses, octopuses, rays and reef sharks.

Kakadu National Park, Northern Territory, ➤ 46–47
With one-third of Australia's bird species, turtles, lizards, snakes, saltwater crocodiles and 10,000 types of insects, Kakadu is a nature-lover's paradise. A number of walking trails lead into the wilderness areas, and tours depart from within the park and from Darwin.

Kangaroo Island, South Australia, ➤ 157
Kangaroos, koalas, seals, goannas and wild geese: Kangaroo Island's parks and reserves protect a diverse range of animals, from both sea and land. You can spot them on a hike (ranging from 2km to 20km/1.2 to 12.5 miles) or on one of the many nature-based tours on offer.

Ningaloo Reef, Western Australia, ➤ 67
This 260km-long (160-mile) coral reef provides one of the world's few opportunities to swim with the oceans' largest fish – the whale shark (Apr–Jul). Giant mantas (May–Nov) and humpback whales (Jul–Nov) are also in residence here, along with turtles and a staggering array of tropical fish accessible just offshore.

Tasmania's World Heritage Area, ➤ 52–53

Being an island, Tasmania's wilderness has largely been spared the ravages of introduced pests, allowing its native species to thrive. There's a good chance of seeing wallabies, wombats and echidnas in any of Tasmania's national parks, especially if you're overnighting. Tasmanian devils are nocturnal, and mostly heard rather than seen (they have a nasty-sounding growl).

Good places to have lunch

Arintji ($$)
A modern Australian café in the heart of the Federation Square precinct.

✉ Federation Square, Melbourne ☎ (03) 9663 9900; www.arintji.com.au
🕐 Lunch and dinner daily 🚃 City Circle tram

Alto ($$$)
Canberra's revolving restaurant offers contemporary cuisine with exceptional views.

✉ Black Mountain Tower, Black Mountain Drive, Acton ☎ (02) 6247 5518;
www.altotower.com.au ⊕ Lunch Thu, Fri and Sun dinner Tue–Sun

City Gardens Café ($–$$)
A delightful café set in Brisbane's lush Botanic Gardens.
✉ City Botanic Gardens, Gardens Point Road, off Alice Street, Brisbane
☎ (07) 3229 1554; www.citygardens.com.au ⊕ Breakfast, lunch and
afternoon tea 🚌 The Loop

Doyle's on the Beach ($$$)
Sydney's most famous seafood restaurant right on the water.
✉ 11 Marine Parade, Watsons Bay, Sydney ☎ (02) 9337 2007;
www.doyles.com.au ⊕ Lunch and dinner daily 🚌 324, 325

Fraser's ($$–$$$)
Modern Australian dining in Perth's parklands.
✉ Fraser's Avenue, Kings Park, West Perth ☎ (08) 9481 7100;
www.frasersrestaurant.com.au ⊕ Breakfast, lunch and dinner daily 🚌 33

Jolleys Boathouse ($$)
Modern Australian food in a delightful setting on the Torrens River.
✉ 1 Jolleys Lane, Adelaide ☎ (08) 8223 2891; www.jolleysboathouse.com
⊕ Lunch Sun–Fri, dinner Mon–Sat

Journal Canteen ($)
Great four-course-and-coffee dégustation in one of the city's
popular lanes.
✉ Upper level, 253 Flinders Lane, Melbourne ☎ (03) 9650 4399
⊕ Mon–Fri noon–4 🚌 Flinders Street

Mures Upper Deck ($$–$$$)
A great seafood menu in the perfect waterfront spot.
✉ Mures Fish Centre, Victoria Dock, Hobart ☎ (03) 6231 1999,
www.mures.com.au ⊕ Lunch and dinner daily

Top activities

Boating: sail a yacht around Queensland's Whitsunday Islands, or go whitewater rafting on the Franklin River (➤ 39).

Bushwalking: there are countless places to go hiking, but try Tasmania (➤ 52–53) and the Blue Mountains (➤ 36–37).

Cross-country skiing: the conditions are ideal around the ski fields of Victoria, Tasmania and New South Wales (Jun–Sep).

Fishing: from trout fishing in Tasmania's lakes to big-game marlin-wrestling off Cairns.

Four-wheel-driving adventures: the Outback's remote, unsealed roads are ideal.

Golf: in Australia golf is a sport for everyone. There are excellent courses everywhere, but those on the Gold Coast are particularly recommended.

Horseback riding: the southeast is ideal – around the Snowy Mountains of NSW and Victoria's alpine areas.

Scuba diving and snorkelling: there is nowhere better than along the Great Barrier Reef.

Surfing: the quintessential Aussie sport – Sydney's coastline, along the Great Ocean Road in Victoria and the Margaret River in Western Australia are all good spots.

Tennis: you will find day/night courts in every major city.

Great views

- From Cottesloe Beach at sunset, Perth.

- From Echo Point in the Blue Mountains, Katoomba.

- From Kings Park over the Swan River and city, Perth.

- From the Southern Star Observation Wheel, Melbourne.

- From Mount Coot-tha, Brisbane.

- From Mount Wellington, Hobart.

- From the Sydney Tower or Skywalk, Sydney.

- From the top of the Sydney Harbour Bridge, Sydney.

- From Black Mountain Tower, Canberra.

- Uluṟu at dawn or dusk, Uluṟu-Kata Tjuṯa National Park.

Exceptional lesser-known destinations

● **Bathurst and Melville islands, Northern Territory:** the home of the Indigenous Tiwi people and their unique culture, ➤ 164.

● **Bunbury, Western Australia:** swim with wild dolphins at the Dolphin Discovery Centre here.

● **Coober Pedy, South Australia:** an opal mining town with most buildings underground.

● **Jervis Bay, New South Wales:** white sands, clear blue waters and unspoiled bushland.

● **Ningaloo Reef, near Exmouth, Western Australia:** the marine life here rivals that of the Great Barrier Reef.

● **Norfolk Island:** an external territory of Australia, packed with fascinating convict and colonial history.

● **Phillip Island, Victoria:** fur seals and fairy penguins.

Good places to stay

NEW SOUTH WALES AND THE AUSTRALIAN CAPITAL TERRITORY

Citigate Central Sydney ($$)

Elegant rooms overlooking Darling Harbour and close to the entertainment district.

✉ 169–179 Thomas Street, Sydney ☎ (02) 9281 6888; www.mirvachotels.com

Peppers Convent ($$$)

One of the Hunter Valley wine region's best hotels, the historic Convent provides spacious rooms that open onto a veranda.

✉ Halls Road, Pokolbin, Hunter Valley ☎ (02) 4993 8999; www.peppers.com.au

Quay Grand Suites ($$$)

In a magnificent location right on Circular Quay, a stone's throw from the Opera House, Harbour Bridge and Botanic Gardens.

✉ 61 Macquarie Street, East Circular Quay, Sydney ☎ (02) 9256 4000; www.mirvachotels.com

QUEENSLAND

M on Mary ($–$$$)

Centrally located, self-contained 1- to 3-bedroom apartments, with a good range of facilities.

✉ 70 Mary Street, Brisbane ☎ (07) 3503 8000; www.monmary.com.au

Reef Palms ($–$$)

Apartment-style accommodation close to The Esplanade, offering standard, deluxe and spa deluxe suites.

✉ 41 Digger Street, Cairns ☎ (07) 4051 2599; www.reefpalms.com.au

VICTORIA
The Langham ($$$)
One of Melbourne's best hotels, this modern establishment rises above the Southgate dining, arts and leisure precinct.
✉ 1 Southgate Avenue, Southbank, Melbourne ☎ (03) 8696 8888

Victoria Hotel ($–$$)
A historic hotel in the heart of Melbourne. Very good value.
✉ 215 Little Collins Street, Melbourne ☎ (03) 9669 0000;
www.victoriahotel.com.au

TASMANIA
Somerset on the Pier ($$$)
A luxurious hotel with loft-style bedrooms. The waterfront setting, on a 1930s pier, is superb.
✉ Elizabeth Street Pier, Hobart ☎ (03) 6220 6600; www.somerset.com

SOUTH AUSTRALIA
Quest Mansions ($–$$)
Spacious self-contained apartments in an historic building close to all the main attractions.
✉ 21 Pulteney Street, Adelaide ☎ (08) 8232 0033;
www.questmansions.com.au

NORTHERN TERRITORY
Novotel Darwin Atrium $$
Overlooking Darwin Harbour, this towering hotel offers spacious rooms and spa facilities.
✉ 100 The Esplanade, Darwin ☎ (08) 8941 0755; www.accorhotels.com.au

WESTERN AUSTRALIA
Ibis Perth ($–$$)
Comfortable rooms in the heart of the city.
✉ 334 Murray Street, Perth ☎ 9322 2844; www.accorhotels.com.au

Places to take the children

NEW SOUTH WALES
Luna Park
You can almost reach out and touch the Harbour Bridge from Luna Park's Ferris wheel. But if fast-whirling rides are what your kids want, it has those too, along with games and all the junk food they could possibly eat.

✉ 1 Olympic Drive, Milsons Point ☎ (02) 9033 7676; www.lunaparksydney.com ⏰ Check website 🚉 Milsons Point Station

Western Plains Zoo
Somewhat off the beaten path (five hours' drive from Sydney), this excellent open-range zoo has over a thousand animals in enclosures replicating their animals' natural habitats. Roar and Snore Zoofari allow kids to to stay overnight and wake up with the animals.

✉ Obley Road, Dubbo ☎ (02) 6881 1400 ⏰ Daily 9–5 🚉 or ✈ Dubbo

QUEENSLAND
Lone Pine Koala Sanctuary
With an all-star cast of Tasmanian devils, echidnas, wombats and native birds, it's the 130 koalas that steal the show. Some will even cuddle-up for a photo.

✉ Jesmond Road, Fig Tree Pocket ☎ (07) 3378 1366 ⏰ Daily 🚌 Nos 430 and 445

Tjapukai Aboriginal Cultural Park
This exciting and educational complex includes dance shows, boomerang-throwing, an art gallery, bush tucker demonstrations and other aspects of indigenous culture.

✉ Kamerunga Road, Smithfield, Cairns ☎ (07) 4042 9900 ⏰ Daily 9–5 and some evenings 🚌 Marlin Coast Sun Bus

VICTORIA
Scienceworks & Planetarium
This complex features interactive displays, performances, screenings and activities for science and space fans of all ages.
✉ 2 Booker Street, Spotswood, Melbourne ☎ (03) 9392 4800 🕓 Daily 10–4:30. Closed Good Fri, 25 Dec 🚉 Spotswood

TASMANIA
Bonorong Wildlife Park
A wildlife park near Hobart, where you can meet Tasmanian devils, wombats, koalas, kangaroos and other native animals.
✉ Briggs Road, Brighton ☎ (03) 6268 1184 🕓 Daily 9–5. Closed 25 Dec
🚌 Tasmanian Redline bus from Hobart

SOUTH AUSTRALIA
St Kilda Adventure Playground
This award-winning beachfront public park has a flying fox ride, spiral slide, monorail and maze.
✉ Fooks Terrace, St Kilda 🕓 Daylight hours ❓ 40 mins north of CBD

NORTHERN TERRITORY
Territory Wildlife Park
Recreating wetlands, woodlands and deserts, this enormous park allows visitors to walk among emus and roos, and observe a vast range of creatures, from quolls to woollybutts.
✉ Cox Peninsula Road, Berry Springs ☎ (08) 8988 7200 🕓 Daily 8:30–6. Closed Christmas Day ❓ 40 mins south of town

WESTERN AUSTRALIA
Rottnest Island
Children will enjoy the sandy beaches, clear waters and cute quokkas – cat-sized kangaroos that roam the island (➤ 180).
✉ Rottnest Island Visitor Centre, Thomson Bay ☎ (08) 9372 9732
🕓 Daily 8–5

Arts, crafts and souvenirs

ABORIGINAL ART AND CRAFT
Gavala Aboriginal Cultural Centre
Sydney outlet specializing in Indigenous art, music and souvenirs.
✉ Shop 131, Harbourside, Darling Harbour, Sydney ☎ (02) 9212 7232

Koorie Heritage Trust
Handmade clapsticks, boomerangs, bush foods (jams and sauces), plus ceramics, music and books. All artists receive royalties and profits go back into the Trust.
✉ 295 King Street, Melbourne ☎ (03) 8622 2600

Maningrida Arts & Culture
The Darwin shopfront for the Arnhem Land arts centre specializing in woven sculptures, jewellery and paintings.
✉ 32 Mitchell Street, Darwin ☎ (08) 8981 4122

Papunya Tula Artists
A gallery owned and directed by Aboriginal people from the Western Desert, selling quality artworks from the region.
✉ 63 Todd Mall, Alice Springs ☎ (08) 8952 4731; www.papunyatula.com.au

Tandanya Aboriginal Cultural Institute
This centre's giftshop is stocked with well-made Aboriginal artworks and artefacts.
✉ 253 Grenfell Street, Adelaide ☎ (08) 8224 3200

AUSTRALIANA
Australian Choice
This shop sells quality Australian-made products, great for gifts and souvenirs.
✉ Canberra Centre, Bunda Street, Canberra City ☎ (02) 6257 5315

Counter
A range of limited-run contemporary homewares, jewellery and objects made by local artisans.
✉ 31 Flinders Lane, Melbourne ☎ (03) 9650 7775

Done Art & Design
Ken Done's colourful Australian designs, printed on beachwear, accessories and housewares.
✉ 123 George Street, The Rocks, Sydney ☎ (02) 9251 6099

Naturally Tasmanian
One of Hobart's best souvenir shops, selling Aussie clothing, sheepskin products, local foodstuffs and much more.
✉ 59 Salamanca Place, Hobart ☎ (03) 6223 4248

RM Williams
The original 'Bushman's Outfitters', where you can buy Akubra hats, Drizabone oilskin coats and country-style clothing.
✉ 389 George Street, Sydney ☎ (02) 9262 2228

around Sydney Opera House, the Botanic Gardens and Macquarie Street

Stroll around the harbour foreshore, visit historic buildings and explore the Art Gallery of NSW.

Start at Circular Quay.

Lively Circular Quay is the focus of the city's ferry system. There are many cafés and shops in the area.

Follow the Circular Quay East walkway towards the Opera House (➤ 50–51).

Take in the exterior of Australia's most famous building, then explore one of the performance halls on a guided tour.

Enter the Botanic Gardens via the gate near the Opera House.

Sydney's Royal Botanic Gardens contain an vast collection of native and imported flora. There are free guided walks daily, and regular special events and exhibits.

After exploring the gardens, continue around the foreshore to the eastern side of the cove.

From Mrs Macquaries Point there are classic views of Sydney Harbour, the Opera House and the Harbour Bridge.

Head south along Mrs Macquaries Road until you reach the Art Gallery.

The Art Gallery of New South Wales is the state's premier gallery, with superb examples of Australian, Aboriginal, European and Asian art. By the gallery is the Domain, a large parkland area.

Follow Art Gallery Road until you reach College Street, then turn right.

Gracious Macquarie Street contains many historic buildings, including the 1819 Hyde Park Barracks, once a home for convicts but now a fascinating museum, and State Parliament House, dating from 1816.

Continue along Macquarie Street, then turn left into Albert Street to return to Circular Quay.

Distance 3km (2 miles)
Time 2–4 hours, depending on stops
Start/end point Circular Quay ✚ *Sydney 3c* ◎ Circular Quay
Lunch Botanic Gardens Restaurant, Café and Kiosk ($–$$)
✉ Royal Botanic Gardens ☎ (02) 9241 2419

Markets

SYDNEY, NEW SOUTH WALES
Glebe Market

A bohemian Saturday market brimming with clothing, music, jewellery and food, best enjoyed in a sunny spot on the grass.

✉ Glebe Public School, corner of Derby Place and Glebe Point Road
🕐 Sat 10–4 ☎ (02) 4237 7499 🚌 431, 433 from central station

Paddington Markets

A vibrant market with over 250 stalls selling clothes, arts and crafts. Good food and free entertainment.

✉ 395 Oxford Street, Paddington ☎ (02) 9331 2923 🕐 Sat 10–4 🚌 378, 380, L82

The Rocks Market

Arts, crafts, jewellery and housewares in the heart of Sydney's tourist mecca.

✉ Upper George Street, The Rocks ☎ (02) 9240 8717 🕐 Sat–Sun 10–5 🚉 Circular Quay

CANBERRA, AUSTRALIAN CAPITAL TERRITORY
Old Bus Depot Markets

On Sundays, this old Canberra bus depot is transformed into a covered market. Handmade goods and collectables are the main items for sale.

✉ 49 Wentworth Avenue, Kingston ☎ (02) 6292 8391 🕐 Sun 10–4 🚌 38, 80

BRISBANE, QUEENSLAND
Eagle Street Pier Craft Market

A Sunday city-centre market offering quality handcrafted goods such as clothes, arts and crafts and some great gifts.

✉ 123 Eagle Street 🕐 Sun 8–4 ☎ (07) 3870 2807 🚌 The Loop

MELBOURNE, VICTORIA
Queen Victoria Market
This Melbourne institution is a large undercover market selling everything from foodstuffs to fashion clothing.

✉ Corner Elizabeth and Victoria streets ☎ (03) 9320 5822 🕐 Daily except Mon and Wed 🚌 Tourist shuttle

St Kilda Esplanade Art and Craft Market
Popular market with around 200 stalls selling handcrafted items.

✉ The Esplanade, St Kilda ☎ (03) 9534 0066 🕐 Sun 10–5 🚌 16, 96

HOBART, TASMANIA
Salamanca Market
The place to be in Hobart on Saturdays – an excellent market, set against the historic backdrop of Salamanca Place.

✉ Salamanca Place ☎ (03) 6238 2843 🕐 Sat 8:30–3 🚌 None

ADELAIDE, SOUTH AUSTRALIA
Central Market
Dating from 1870, this is mainly a produce market – but a fascinating place to wander around nonetheless.

✉ Grote and Gouger Streets ☎ (08) 8203 7203 🕐 Tue, Thu–Sat. Closed public holidays 🚌 City Loop

DARWIN, NORTHERN TERRITORY
Mindil Beach Sunset Markets
An evening market with arts, crafts, food and free entertainment.

✉ Mindil Beach 🕐 May–Oct, Thu 5–10 and Sun 4–9 🚌 None

FREMANTLE, WESTERN AUSTRALIA
Fremantle Markets
A National Trust-classified indoor market that sells fresh produce, clothing and crafts.

✉ 84 South Terrace ☎ (08) 9335 2515 🕐 Fri–Sun 🚆 Fremantle

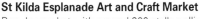

Exploring

Australia is a young nation in an ancient land. Its people are from diverse backgrounds: indigenous Australian ancestry dates back thousands of years, while many other Australians arrived more recently – almost a quarter of the population was born overseas.

Although famous for its pioneering history and Outback traditions, around three-quarters of the population is clustered together along the coast, in well-developed towns and cities. It's roughly the same size as Europe, but Australia's population is 30 times smaller, leaving a lot of uninhabited land to explore.

The vast Australian landscape varies from lush tropical rainforests to arid deserts, and snow-capped alpine peaks to long stretches of sandy beach. Wherever you go, the scenery is spectacular, and there's more to see just a little further on…

New South Wales and the Australian Capital Territory

New South Wales, named by Cook in 1770 because it reminded him of South Wales, is Australia's fourth-largest state but has the largest population – over 6.7 million. Geographically, it is 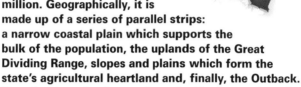 **made up of a series of parallel strips: a narrow coastal plain which supports the bulk of the population, the uplands of the Great Dividing Range, slopes and plains which form the state's agricultural heartland and, finally, the Outback. The climate varies from subtropical in the north to the winter snows of the mountains in the far south.**

Although within the boundaries of New South Wales, the Australian Capital Territory, or ACT, is governed and administered separately. The territory and the national capital, Canberra, were created early in the 20th century to resolve the long-running rivalry between Sydney and Melbourne over which city should be the nation's capital.

www.visitnsw.com.au

SYDNEY

The nation's birthplace has developed from its humble convict beginnings into a vibrant metropolis that holds its own on the world stage. With a multicultural population of over 4.25 million, Sydney is the continent's largest and, many would say, most brash, city. Although the pace of life is faster here than anywhere else in Australia, Sydneysiders still know how to relax – the city's harbour, long golden beaches and surrounding bushland make sure of that.

Sydney has truly come of age as a major city and an enviable tourist destination. It has been voted 'the world's best city' by discerning travellers the world over, but perhaps the biggest accolade came when Sydney was chosen as the host city for the 2000 Summer Olympic Games. In addition to the fascinating convict history, museums, galleries and, of course, the 'Great Outdoors', the city offers wonderful shopping, an innovative and highly acclaimed restaurant scene and a wide choice of nightlife.

Although visitors spend most of their time in the inner city and eastern suburbs, an entirely different world lies beyond. To the north lie the glorious Northern Beaches with surf, sand and a far more relaxed lifestyle, the charming waterway of Pittwater, and the bushland of Ku-ring-gai Chase National Park. To the west, you can visit historic Parramatta and Sydney Olympic Park, the Olympic Games site. Sydney's inner suburbs also have a great deal to offer. A visit to famous Bondi, Manly or one of the many other beaches is a must.

www.sydney.com

✚ 23J

Australian Museum

A world-class natural history museum, this is an excellent place to learn about pre-European Aboriginal life and Australia's native fauna. Also featured are exhibits on human evolution, minerals, dinosaurs, biodiversity and a fascinating skeletons room.

www.austmus.gov.au

🏁 *Sydney 4f* ✉ 6 College Street ☎ (02) 9320 6000 🕐 Daily 9:30–5. Closed 25 Dec 💵 Moderate

Darling Harbour

With its harbourside shopping and eating complexes, the delightful Chinese Garden, the IMAX Theatre and National Maritime Museum, Darling Harbour is one of Sydney's most popular recreation areas. One of the best attractions here is the **Sydney Aquarium,** where you will encounter sharks, crocodiles and colourful Great Barrier Reef fish at close quarters. The nearby

futuristic building of the Australian National Maritime Museum contains several galleries covering maritime themes as diverse as the discovery of Australia and surfboard technology. Many of the exhibits are interactive. Moored outside are various vessels, including a World War II destroyer and a submarine.

www.darlingharbour.com

🏁 *Sydney 2f* ✉ Darling Harbour
☎ (02) 9240 8788

Sydney Aquarium

☎ (02) 8251 7800 🕐 Daily 9–10 (last admission at 9) 💵 Expensive
🚉 Monorail Darling Park

Powerhouse Museum

Sydney's largest museum is an entertaining technological and cultural wonderland with everything from a huge 18th-century steam engine and a 1930s art deco cinema to holograms and irresistible hands-on displays.
www.phm.gov.au

✚ *Sydney 2g* ✉ 500 Harris Street, Ultimo
☎ (02) 9217 0111 ⏰ Daily 10–5. Closed 25 Dec
✋ Moderate

The Rocks

With its intriguing past and prime harbourside location, this is Sydney's tourist mecca. It was the site of Australia's first 'village' and has had a colourful history. In addition to wandering the narrow streets, sitting on the waterfront and browsing in the many shops, Rocks highlights are a lively weekend market and several small museums – including the Sydney Observatory at nearby Millers Point. Full details of the area are available from the Information Centre.
www.therocks.com

🕇 *Sydney 3b* 🚇 Circular Quay
ℹ️ Sydney Visitor Centre ✉️ Corner of Argyle and
Playfair streets, The Rocks ☎ (02) 9240 8788
🕐 Daily 9:30–5:30. Closed Good Fri and 25 Dec

Sydney Harbour
Best places to see, ➤ 50–51.

Sydney Harbour Bridge
Completed in 1932, this famous bridge is still
the primary link between the harbour's north
and south shores, although the Harbour Tunnel
handles a large share of the traffic. Take the
walkway from the Rocks, and climb the 200
steps of the Pylon Lookout, with stunning
views over the Harbour and Opera House. Or,
teeter along catwalks and up ladders to walk
along the Bridge's upper arch with BridgeClimb.
🕇 *Sydney 3a* ☎ Pylon Lookout: (02) 9240 1100;
BridgeClimb: (02) 8274 7777; www.bridgeclimb.com
🕐 Lookout and Museum: daily 10–5. Closed 25 Dec
✋ Lookout: inexpensive; BridgeClimb: expensive
🚇 Circular Quay

Sydney Opera House
Best places to see, ➤ 50–51.

Sydney Tower
The best view is from the top of this 304.8m (1,000ft) tower. From the observation level there are superb 360-degree views of the city and its surroundings. The tower has a revolving restaurant, particularly spectacular at night. The more adventurous might like to try the Skywalk, which involves being harnessed to the edge of a moving, glass-floored platform outside the tower for 45 minutes.

www.sydneytower.com.au

✚ *Sydney 3e* ✉ 100 Market Street ☎ (02) 9333 9222; 🕐 Tower: Sun–Fri 9–10:30, Sat 9 –11:30; Skywalk: daily 9:30–8:45 🖐 Moderate–expensive

Taronga Zoo
Reached by a scenic ferry ride, Taronga is visited as much for its harbourside location as for the opportunity to meet native Australian wildlife. There are koalas, kangaroos, echidnas, wombats and Tasmanian devils here, as well as native birds and reptiles, and a large collection of other zoo animals.

www.zoo.nsw.gov.au

✚ *Sydney 3a (off map)* ✉ Bradleys Head Road, Mosman ☎ (02) 9969 2777 🕐 Daily 9–5 🖐 Expensive 🍴 Cafés ($$) and kiosk ($) 🚌 247 ⛴ From Circular Quay

CANBERRA AND THE AUSTRALIAN CAPITAL TERRITORY (ACT)

Created out of New South Wales farmland after its site was designated in 1908, Canberra is a planned city unlike anywhere else in the nation. Designed by American architect Walter Burley Griffin, and surrounded by parks and gardens, the national capital is a pleasant environment. Canberra is the home of Australia's Federal government; 40 per cent of the 329,000 population is employed in this field. The city is full of diplomatic missions and government departments, and – appealing for the visitor – national museums and galleries. The central focus is Lake Burley Griffin, a location for cruises, from where roads radiate to suburbs and wild bushland. Beyond the city, the surrounding Australian Capital Territory offers rugged Namadgi National Park, Tidbinbilla Nature Reserve and historic Lanyon Homestead.

www.visitcanberra.com.au ✚ 23K

Australian National Botanic Gardens

Containing the world's best collection of unique Australian flora, these gardens feature more than 600 species of eucalyptus trees, a rock garden, the delightful rainforest gully, and a Tasmanian alpine garden. Self-guided arrow trails make it easy to find your way around.

Looming behind the gardens is Black Mountain (779m/2,555ft), capped by the futuristic Black Mountain Tower. There is a spectacular view of the city and surrounds from the tower's viewing gallery.

www.anbg.gov.au

✉ Clunies Ross Street, Acton ☎ (02) 6250 9450 🕐 Mon–Fri 8:30–5, Sat–Sun 8:30–6 (till 8pm Jan) 🎫 Free 🍴 Café ($–$$) 🚌 81 ❓ Free guided walks 11am and 2pm daily

Australian War Memorial

In a dramatic location at the head of Anzac Parade, this impressive monument and museum commemorates the Australians who served in various wars. Its many thousands of displays include aeroplanes, tanks, guns, military memorabilia and artworks.

www.awm.gov.au

✉ Treloar Crescent, Campbell ☎ (02) 6243 4211 🕐 Daily 10–5. Closed 25 Dec 🎫 Free 🍴 Cafés ($–$$) 🚌 10, 930

National Gallery of Australia

This is the nation's premier gallery, and the ideal place to view good examples of Aboriginal and Australian art. European, Asian and American artworks are also featured, and the gallery hosts excellent travelling exhibitions.

www.nga.gov.au

✉ Parkes Place, Parkes ☎ (02) 6240 6501 🕑 Daily 10–5. Closed 25 Dec ✋ Free

National Museum of Australia

This modern museum explores the key issues, events and people that have shaped Australia. The themed galleries employ state-of-the-art technology and feature the symbols of the nation, indigenous peoples, and stories of ordinary and famous Australians.

www.nma.gov.au

✉ Lawson Crescent, Acton Peninsula ☎ (02) 6208 5000 🕑 Daily 9–5 ✋ Free general entry 🚌 3, 934, 981

Parliament House

Canberra's architectural and political centrepiece was completed in 1988, at a staggering cost of over $1,000 million. It contains the House of Representatives and the Senate, and features fine artworks and craftsmanship. Guided tours are available, and the view from the roof is superb. Also in this Parliamentary Triangle area stands the more modest 1927 Old Parliament House, now housing the National Portrait Gallery.

www.aph.gov.au

✉ Capital Hill ☎ (02) 6277 5399 🕑 Daily 9–5 (later when Parliament is sitting). Closed 25 Dec

 Free Café ($–$$) 31, 34, 39
45-min guided tours, every 30 mins

Questacon

Also known as The National
Science and Technology Centre,
this exciting, modern complex
brings the world of science alive.
Education and entertainment are
combined brilliantly in the 170 or
so interactive exhibits.
www.questacon.edu.au
King Edward Terrace, Parkes (02)
6270 2800 Daily 9–5. Closed 25 Dec
Moderate

More to see in New South Wales

BLUE MOUNTAINS
Best places to see, ➤ 36–37.

BROKEN HILL
Broken Hill's harsh landscape is far removed from the waterside ambience of Sydney. This silver-mining town in far western NSW is a good Outback destination. Here you can tour one of the mines, visit the Royal Flying Doctor Service base, and take a trip to nearby Kinchega National Park or the ghost town of Silverton.
www.visitbrokenhill.com.au
🏕 20J 🚌 🚇 ✖ From Sydney ℹ Broken Hill Visitor Centre ✉ Blende Street ☎ (08) 8080 3560 🕐 Daily 8:30–5

BYRON BAY
With a wonderful climate, sandy beaches and pounding surf, 'Byron' attracts surfers, scuba-divers and holidaymakers in droves. Walk to Cape Byron (Australia's most easterly point), enjoy fine restaurants, or just browse the art and craft shops. Take a drive to the hinterland rainforests or the nearby town of Mullumbimby.
www.visitbyronbay.com
🏕 24H ✖ Ballina or Coolangatta, then a drive ℹ Byron Bay Visitor Centre ✉ 80 Jonson Street ☎ (02) 6680 8558 🕐 Daily 9–5

COFFS HARBOUR
Tourism and banana growing are the main industries of this coastal city, which offers excellent beaches and a sunny climate. Kids will enjoy the Pet Porpoise Pool and Big Banana leisure park, while a drive inland to the picturesque town of Bellingen and rainforests of World Heritage-listed Dorrigo National Park is recommended.
www.coffscoast.com.au
🏕 24H 🚌 🚇 or ✖ From Sydney ℹ Coffs Coast Visitor Centre ✉ Corner Pacific Highway and Maclean streets ☎ (02) 6652 1522 🕐 Daily 9–5

a drive in the Blue Mountains

Explore one of Sydney's favourite recreation areas: the rugged and scenic Blue Mountains.

From central Sydney, go west (towards the Olympic Park) along Parramatta Road to join the Western Motorway (M4). Continue on to the Great Western Highway (Route 32) at the base of the mountains.

After Glenbrook (information centre), continue to the Norman Lindsay Gallery and Museum at Faulconbridge, devoted to one of Australia's most celebrated artists and writers. Further on, Wentworth Falls offers short bushwalks and the Falls Reserve.

Continue on the highway until you reach the Leura turn-off (approximately 2 hours' drive from Sydney).

The picturesque town of Leura has cafés, crafts shops and the historic Everglades Gardens.

Take the signposted scenic Cliff Drive to nearby Katoomba.

This brings you to Echo Point, with spectacular views of the Three Sisters rock formation, the surrounding cliffs and the forested Jamison Valley.

Continue on the Cliff Drive, which rejoins the Great Western Highway. Follow the signs to Blackheath.

In Blackheath, head for the National Parks and Wildlife Service Heritage Centre, and a splendid panorama.

Keep following the Great Western Highway to Mount Victoria.

Mount Victoria is classifed as an Urban Conservation Area and has a museum, teashops and a few antiques shops.

Follow the Darling Causeway, then turn right onto the Bells Line of Road.

Visit Mount Tomah Botanic Garden, the cool-climate branch of Sydney's Royal Botanic Gardens.

Continue to Windsor, then follow Route 40 and the Western Motorway.

Distance 280km (174 miles)
Time A full day, or stay overnight if possible
Start/end point George Street, central Sydney ✚ *Sydney 3h*
Lunch Café Bon Ton (➤ 102)

HUNTER VALLEY

Wine and wineries are the main attraction of
this large river valley northwest of Sydney,
centred around the town of Cessnock and the village of Pokolbin.
Grapes have been cultivated here since the 1830s and there are
now over 100 wineries in the region; many of these can be toured
and you can, of course, sample the fine wines by visiting their
Cellar Door. The Hunter also has a reputation for excellent
accommodation and dining, making it a very popular weekend
destination for Sydneysiders.

www.winecountry.com.au

✚ 23J 🚉 Maitland, then a bus to Cessnock

🛈 Hunter Valley Wine Country Visitor Centre ✉ 455 Wine Country Drive,
Pokolbin ☎ (02) 4990 0900 🕐 Mon–Sat 9–5, Sun 9–4

KIAMA

One of the closest South Coast resorts to Sydney, the small town
of Kiama (90 minutes' drive away) has long enjoyed great

popularity. As well as good beaches and surfing, the town has a famous blowhole, discovered by whaler George Bass in 1797 on a voyage of coastal exploration, and many historic buildings. Kiama is close to the charmingly rural Kangaroo Valley, and the Minnamurra Rainforest Centre within the Budderoo National Park.

www.kiama.com.au

✚ 23K 🚆 From Sydney

ℹ Kiama Visitor Centre ✉ Blowhole Point ☎ (02) 4232 3322

🕓 Daily 9–5. Closed 25 Dec

LORD HOWE ISLAND

A true South Sea paradise. Dominated by sheer peaks, this World Heritage-listed small island is just 11km (7 miles) long and 2.8km (1.7 miles) at its widest. The high peaks and lower, scattered hills were created by volcanic activity, and below these lie kentia palm forests, idyllic sandy beaches, a fringing coral reef, and the clear blue waters of the island's lagoon, home to over 500 fish species.

www.lordhoweisland.info

✚ 24J (off map) ✈ From Sydney and Brisbane

ℹ Island Visitor Centre ☎ 1800 240 937 or (02) 6563 2114 🕓 Mon–Fri 9:30–2:30, Sun 9:30–2 ❓ Various grades of accommodation available

MYALL LAKES NATIONAL PARK

This North Coast national park encompasses both a chain of large freshwater lakes and an idyllic 40km (25-mile) coastline. You can rent a houseboat or canoe to explore the lakes, or camp and enjoy surfing and swimming off the golden beaches. The area is particularly appealing to birdwatchers and bushwalkers.

www.environment.nsw.gov.au/nationalparks.htm

✚ 23J ☎ 1300 361 967 or (02) 9995 5000 ⏱ Daily ✋ Inexpensive

❓ No public transport into the park

SNOWY MOUNTAINS

In the state's far south, reached via the town of Jindabyne, this upland region encompasses Kosciuszko National Park, where you can ski in winter from the resorts of Thredbo and Perisher Blue. The wilderness park contains heathland and alpine vegetation, as well as Mount Kosciuszko, Australia's highest point (just 2,228m/7,310ft). In summer the area is great for bushwalking, trout fishing, horseback riding and mountain biking.

www.snowymountains.com.au

🚻 22K ✉ Snowy Region Visitor Centre, Kosciuszko Road, Jindabyne
☎ (02) 6450 5600 🕓 Winter daily 8–5:30; summer daily 8:30–5
🚌 Jindabyne and Thredbo.
Perisher Blue (ski season)

SOUTHERN HIGHLANDS
Just 100km (62 miles) from Sydney, this upland region offers a blend of rugged Australian bush, rolling English-type farmland and genteel townships.

Colonial history is well represented: the charming village of Berrima dates from the early 1830s and is full of historic buildings. You can shop for crafts and antiques in Berrima, Moss Vale and Bowral, and go bushwalking in the Morton National Park.
www.southern-highlands.com.au
🚻 23K 🚆 Mittagong, Bowral, Moss Vale, Exeter, Bundanoon
ℹ Information Centre ✉ 62–70 Main Street, Mittagong ☎ 1300 657 559 or (02) 4871 2888 🕓 Mon–Fri 9–5, Sat–Sun 9–4

HOTELS

NEW SOUTH WALES
SYDNEY
Citigate Central Sydney ($$)
See page 68.

Hotel Ibis Darling Harbour ($$)
Great views, a popular restaurant and a waterfront location.
✉ 70 Murray Street, Darling Harbour ☎ (02) 9563 0888;
www.hotelibisdarlingharbour.com.au 🚈 Monorail or light rail to Convention

Park Hyatt Sydney ($$$)
One of Sydney's very best hotels, opposite the Opera House.
✉ 7 Hickson Road, The Rocks ☎ (02) 9241 1234;
www.sydney.park.hyatt.com 🚉 Circular Quay

Quay Grand Suites ($$$)
See page 68.

The Russell ($–$$)
Small Victorian hotel with a roof garden, close to the city centre.
✉ 143a George Street, The Rocks ☎ (02) 9241 3543;
www.therussell.com.au 🚊 Circular Quay

BLUE MOUNTAINS
The Mountain Heritage ($$–$$$)
Historic hotel in an ideal location, with superb views and a range of
good-value accommodation.
✉ Corner of Apex and Lovel streets, Katoomba ☎ (02) 4782 2155;
www.mountainheritage.com.au 🚈 Katoomba

COFFS HARBOUR
BreakFree Aanuka Beach Resort ($$–$$$)
This attractive beachfront hotel offers a range of suites set in
delightful gardens.
✉ 11 Firman Drive, Diggers Beach ☎ (02) 6652 7555;
www.breakfree.com.au

HUNTER VALLEY
Peppers Convent ($$$)
See page 68.

AUSTRALIAN CAPITAL TERRITORY
CANBERRA
Forrest Inn and Apartments ($–$$)
Good-value rooms and self-contained serviced apartments close to
Parliament House and within walking distance of most attractions.
✉ 30 National Circuit, Forrest ☎ (02) 6295 3433;
www.forrestinn.com.au 🚌 39

Hyatt Hotel Canberra ($$$)
The capital's finest hotel, close to the main attractions. A charming
1920s building, with well-maintained gardens in which to relax.
✉ Commonwealth Avenue, Yarralumla ☎ (02) 6270 1234;
www.canberra.park.hyatt.com 🚌 2, 3, 934

RESTAURANTS
NEW SOUTH WALES
SYDNEY
Berowra Waters Inn ($$$)
In a stunning location surrounded by bushland on the Hawkesbury
River, and serving excellent Modern Australian food.
✉ Near Public Ferry Terminal, Berowa Waters ☎ (02) 9456 1027;
www.berowrawatersinn.com 🍴 Lunch Fri–Sun, dinner Thu–Sat 🚌 None,
overland access by car ✈ Seaplane from Rosebay

Doyle's on the Beach ($$$)
See page 61.

Longrain ($–$$)
This slick, modern, industrial warehouse space does Thai-inspired
communal dining. No dinner bookings, so arrive early.
✉ 85 Commonwealth Street, Surry Hills ☎ (02) 9280 2888;
www.longrain.com 🍴 Lunch Mon–Fri, dinner daily 🚉 Central Station

Rockpool ($$$)

Sydney's celebrated special-occasion seafood restaurant, noted for its sustainable choices, inspirational dishes and surroundings.

✉ 107 George Street, The Rocks ☎ (02) 9252 1888; www.rockpoolsydney.com ◷ Lunch Mon–Fri, dinner Mon–Sat 🚉 The Circular Quay

Tetsuya's ($$$)

French, Japanese and Australian fusion in a high-class setting.

✉ 529 Kent Street ☎ (02) 9267 2900; www.tetsuyas.com ◷ Lunch Sat, dinner Tue–Sat 🚉 Town Hall

BLUE MOUNTAINS
Café Bon Ton ($–$$)

A quaint café in the lovely mountain village of Leura.

✉ 192 The Mall, Leura ☎ (02) 4782 4377; www.bonton.com.au ◷ Breakfast, lunch and dinner daily 🚉 Leura

Solitary Restaurant & Kiosk ($–$$$)

The restaurant's exquisite French-leaning dishes are served in a magnificent cottage overlooking a sweeping valley and mountain scene. The kiosk serves café fare in an equally spectacular setting.

✉ 90 Cliff Drive, Leura ☎ (02) 4782 1164; www.solitary.com.au ◷ Restaurant: lunch Sat–Sun, dinner Wed–Sun; kiosk: brunch and lunch daily

BYRON BAY
Rae's on Watego ($$$)

This romantic resort restaurant offers outdoor dining on the beachfront, and a Thai-infused menu.

✉ 8 Marine Parade ☎ (02) 6685 5366; www.raes.com.au ◷ Lunch and dinner Oct–Mar; dinner Apr–Sep

AUSTRALIAN CAPITAL TERRITORY
CANBERRA
Alto ($$$)

See pages 60–61.

Gus' Cafe ($)

A tiny Canberra institution. Excellent coffee, snacks and café fare.

✉ Shop 8, Garema Place, Bunda Street, Canberra City ☎ (02) 6248 8118

🕓 Breakfast, lunch and dinner daily 🚌 Any city-centre bus

SHOPPING

ABORIGINAL ART
Artery

Contemporary paintings from indigenous artists across Australia.

✉ 221 Darlinghurst Road, Darlinghurst ☎ (02) 9380 8234 🚇 Kings Cross

Gavala Aboriginal Cultural Centre

See page 72.

OPALS, GEMS AND JEWELLERY
Flame Opals

One of Sydney's best opal retailers. Offers a good range of stones, both unset and made up into fine jewellery.

✉ 119 George Street, The Rocks, Sydney ☎ (02) 9247 3446 🚉 Circular Quay

Percy Marks Fine Gems

One of Sydney's oldest gem specialists. Opals, Argyle diamonds and South Sea pearls all set in handcrafted Australian jewellery.

✉ 60 Elizabeth Street, Sydney ☎ (02) 9233 1355 🚇 Martin Place

DEPARTMENT STORES AND SHOPPING CENTRES
David Jones

One of Australia's very best stores, glamorous 'DJs' operates from two enormous city-centre buildings.

✉ Elizabeth Street and Market Street, Sydney ☎ (02) 9266 5544
🚇 St James

Queen Victoria Building

A vast and delightful 1890s building with over 200 boutiques.

✉ Corner of George, York and Market streets, Sydney ☎ (02) 9264 9209
🚇 Town Hall

ENTERTAINMENT

NIGHTLIFE

The Entertainment Quarter, Fox Studios

Cinemas, markets (Wed, Sat, Sun), shops, bars and eateries.
✉ 122 Lang Road, Moore Park, Sydney ☎ (02) 8117 6700;
www.eqmoorepark.com.au 🚌 373, 374, 376, 377, 391, 392, 394, 396,
397, 399

Home

A popular nightclub on the waterfront. Bars, dining and dancing.
✉ Cockle Bay Wharf, Darling Harbour, Sydney ☎ (02) 9266 0600;
www.homesydney.com 🕓 Daily 🚝 Monorail to Darling Park

Star City Casino

Comprising 200 gaming tables, two cinemas, seven restaurants,
a hotel and a nightclub.
✉ 80 Pyrmont Street, Pyrmont ☎ (02) 9777 9000; www.starcity.com.au
🕓 24 hours daily 🚝 Light Rail to Star City

THEATRE AND CLASSICAL ENTERTAINMENT

Belvoir St Theatre

An inner-city theatre often showing contemporary Australian plays.
✉ 25 Belvoir Street, Surry Hills, Sydney ☎ (02) 9699 3444;
www.belvoir.com.au 🚉 Central

Canberra Theatre Centre

Canberra's main arts venue, for regular opera, ballet and theatre.
✉ Civic Square, London Circuit, Canberra City ☎ (02) 6275 2700;
www.canberratheatre.org.au 🚌 Any city-centre bus

Sydney Theatre Company

Sydney's premier company puts on over a dozen plays each year.
✉ Pier 4, Hickson Road, Walsh Bay ☎ (02) 9250 1777;
www.sydneytheatre.com.au 🚉 Circular Quay, then 20-min walk

Sydney Opera House

See pages 50–51.

Queensland

**Occupying an enormous chunk of the
continent's northeast, Queensland is the
second largest state after Western
Australia. From the subtropical capital of
Brisbane in the south, this vast tract of
land – much of which has a hot,
sunny and virtually winterless
climate – stretches north to
well within the tropics.**

Cairns

Brisbane

Many people come here solely
to experience the Great Barrier
Reef World Heritage Site, a
magnificent natural wonder that
lies parallel to the coast's sandy beaches and idyllic islands. But
Queensland offers much more. Behind the coastal strip and the
hills of the Great Dividing Range, stretches the untamed Outback,
while in the far north are lush tropical rainforests and the country's
northernmost tip, the Cape York Peninsula.

www.queenslandholidays.com.au

BRISBANE

Brisbane has come a long way. What began in 1824 as a penal outpost of New South Wales has become a thoroughly desirable destination. Brisbane is among the country's fastest growing cities, appealing for its seemingly incongruous combination of ritz and laid-back atmosphere. With a subtropical climate, it has a slower pace of life than that of southern cities, and Queensland's capital has blossomed into a most attractive metropolis.

Although most visitors do not linger for long in Brisbane before heading south to the Gold Coast or north to the attractions of the coast and Great Barrier Reef, there is plenty to see and do here. The city's riverside location is an important ingredient in its charm: Brisbane stands on a sweeping bend of the Brisbane River, and a leisurely cruise or ferry ride is a highlight of any trip.

There are museums, galleries and a few graceful old buildings here, but sunny Brisbane is a largely modern city, concerned for the most part with relaxing and enjoying the good things in life. The brilliantly designed South Bank parklands, which include a swimming lagoon and sandy beach, and the city's many parks and gardens, are ideal places to indulge in such pursuits, as are the islands and beaches of nearby Moreton Bay. You can also explore the pleasant city centre – particularly the shops and outdoor cafés of Queen Street Mall; the Riverside Centre and its ferry wharves, just off Eagle Street; and the Roma Street Parkland.

www.ourbrisbane.com

➕ 24H

City Botanic Gardens

Brisbane's premier gardens are in a delightful riverside setting and provide the ideal spot for a break from sightseeing and the heat. The gardens are open around the clock. Wander among the palm trees, Bunya pines and rainforest area, or take a guided walk.

✉ Alice Street ☎ (07) 3027 4384 🍴 City Gardens Café (▶ 61) 🖐 Free
🚌 The Loop

Mount Coot-Tha

It's worth making the trip to this peak, 6.5km (4 miles) from the city centre, especially at night, for the wonderful view of Brisbane and its surroundings.

You can visit the **Brisbane Botanic Gardens,** with their tropical and native flora, hiking paths and Aboriginal trails, as well as the Planetarium, with telescopes and a skydome onto which a dramatic image of the southern sky is projected.

www.brisbanelookout.com

Brisbane Botanic Gardens

✉ Mount Coot-tha Road, Toowong
☎ (07) 3403 2535 ⊙ Sep–Mar daily 8–5:30 ; Apr–Aug daily 8–5 ⊘ Gardens: free; Skydome: moderate 🍴 Café ($); restaurant ($$) 🚌 471

Queensland Cultural Centre

This modern South Bank complex includes two important museums –

the Queensland Art Gallery, with its fine collection of Australian, Aboriginal, Asian, Pacific and European art; and the Queensland Museum with some particularly good Aboriginal and natural history displays.

Nearby to the south, the large riverside South Bank Parklands is one of Australia's best urban parks, with bars, pubs, restaurants and cafés, shopping, an IMAX theatre and weekend markets. The **Queensland Maritime Museum** is also worth a visit.

www.south-bank.net.au

✉ Corner of Melbourne and Grey streets, South Brisbane ☎ Art Gallery: (07) 3840 7303; www.qag.qld.gov.au. Museum: (07) 3840 7555; www.qm.qld.gov.au 🕔 Art Gallery: Mon–Fri 10–5, Sat–Sun 9–5. Museum 9:30–5 ✋ Free

Queensland Maritime Museum

✉ Stanley Street ☎ (07) 3844 5361 🕔 Daily 9:30–4:30, last entry 3:30

Queensland Sciencentre

With around 100 hands-on exhibits, this is the state's largest science and technology centre. Even the most non-scientific mind, young or old, will be captivated, and special shows and demonstrations are held daily.

✉ Queensland Museum, corner of Melbourne and Grey streets, South Brisbane ☎ (07) 3840 7555 🕔 Daily 9:30–5 ✋ Moderate

More to see in Queensland

CARNARVON GORGE NATIONAL PARK

Although it is very remote (over 250km/155 miles from the nearest town, Roma), a visit to this spectacular park is well rewarded. The Carnarvon Creek has cut through soft sandstone to create 200m (655ft) cliffs and a 30km (18-mile) long gorge. There is some good bushwalking, as well as lush vegetation and ancient Aboriginal paintings. Check road conditions before setting out.

www.epa.qld.gov.au

🚩 11E ✉ Carnarvon National Park, via Rolleston ☎ (07) 4984 4505
🕐 Daily ✋ Free ❌ Roma, then a drive

CAIRNS AND DISTRICT
Best places to see, ➤ 38–39.

CHARTERS TOWERS
Once the second largest city in Queensland, with its own stock exchange, this historic town, situated 135km (84 miles) west of Townsville, was built on gold over a century ago. Today it is a living museum of grand hotels, banks and other National Trust-classified buildings. The World Theatre, built in 1891 as an international bank, now serves as a focus for arts and entertainment with a fully restored auditorium, cinema, archival centre and art gallery.

The town has a number of significant events each year, including the Australia Day (26 January) Cricket Festival, and one of Australia's largest country music festivals on the May Day weekend with Australian Bush Poetry Championships and a ute muster. (See also Townsville ➤ 116.)

www.charterstowers.qld.gov.au

✚ 10D 🚌 or ✕ Townsville

ℹ Visitor Information Centre ✉ 74 Mosman Street ☎ (07) 4761 5533

🕐 Daily 9–5. Closed Good Fri, 25–26 Dec, 1 Jan

FRASER ISLAND

At 121km (75 miles) long, this extraordinary World Heritage Site is the world's largest sand island. Yet with extensive rainforest, over 40 freshwater lakes, long sandy beaches and strangely coloured sand cliffs this is a surprisingly varied environment. The wildlife – including dingoes and wallabies – is prolific, making the island the perfect destination for nature lovers and birdwatchers. Fraser Island is reached by vehicular ferry and a four-wheel-drive vehicle is necessary, unless taking one of the many tours.

www.queenslandholidays.com.au

➕ 12E 🖐 Free 🚢 From Hervey Bay 🛈 Hervey Bay Tourism ✉ Corner of Urraween and Maryborough Hervey Bay roads, Hervey Bay ☎ 1800 811 728 or (07) 4125 9855 🕐 Daily 9–5. Closed Good Friday and 25 Dec

GOLD COAST
Best places to see, ➤ 40–41.

GREAT BARRIER REEF
Best places to see, ➤ 42–43.

LAMINGTON NATIONAL PARK

Temperate and subtropical rainforests, wild mountain scenery with waterfalls, gorges, rock pools, caves and abundant wildlife all combine to make this World Heritage-listed national park a must-see destination for nature lovers. There are 160km (100 miles) of hiking paths to explore, as well as plenty of easy trails and a rainforest canopy trail. The most accessible and popular sections of the national park are Green Mountains and Binna Burra.
www.epa.qld.gov.au

✚ 24H 👆 Free ✖ Gold Coast or Brisbane, then a drive

ℹ Green Mountains ☎ (07) 5544 0634; Binna Burra ☎ (07) 5533 3584

LONGREACH

Longreach in Queensland's Outback was the first home of the national airline Qantas (Queensland and Northern Territory Aerial Services) during the 1920s, and the town has many charming old buildings. The major attraction is the excellent **Australian Stockman's Hall of Fame** and Outback Heritage Centre – a modern complex that pays tribute to the early explorers, pioneers and settlers.

✚ 10E

Australian Stockman's Hall of Fame

✉ Landsborough Highway, Longreach ☎ (07) 4658 2166; www.outbackheritage.com.au

🕑 Daily 9–5. Closed 25 Dec 👋 Expensive

🍴 Snack bar ($) 🚌 Longreach

SUNSHINE COAST

Stretching for 65km (40 miles)
to the north of Brisbane, the
Sunshine Coast region has
beautiful white beaches, low-
key resorts, and some
outstanding national parks. The
stylish main resort town of
Noosa Heads offers sandy
beaches and cosmopolitan
dining. Nearby attractions
include Steve Irwin's Australia
Zoo, and exploring the dunes
and coloured sand cliffs of
Cooloola National Park. Inland,
you can tour the Blackall
Range region, where there are
green hills, charming villages
and rich farming country.
www.sunshinecoast.org

✚ 12E ✖ Sunshine Coast
ℹ Tourist Information ✉ Hastings
Street, Noosa Heads ☎ (07) 5430
5000 🕐 Daily 9–5. Closed 25 Dec

TOWNSVILLE

With a population of about 145,000, this historic harbourside settlement is Australia's largest tropical city. The main points of interest are the excellent Reef HQ aquarium complex, the Museum of Tropical Queensland housing a replica of the wreck HMS *Pandora*, and the wildlife-rich Billabong Sanctuary. You can visit nearby Magnetic Island, with its fine beaches and abundant wildlife, and take trips to the Great Barrier Reef.

www.townsvilleonline.com.au

🚌 10D 🚆 or ✈ Townsville

ℹ Visitor Centre ✉ Flinders Mall ☎ (07) 4721 3660

🕐 Mon–Fri 9–5, Sat–Sun 9–1

WHITSUNDAY ISLANDS

Reached via Proserpine and the villages of
Airlie Beach and Shute Harbour, these
central coast islands form a very popular
holiday destination. There are over 70
islands, mostly hilly and forested, with
exquisite beaches and incredibly clear
turquoise waters. There is a good choice
of resorts – from high-class Hayman to
the less sophisticated national park Long
Island resort. There are plenty of day trips
to the reef, and the region is perfect for
sailing, snorkelling and water sports.

www.whitsundaytourism.com

✚ 11D ✖ Proserpine

ℹ Whitsunday Information Centre ✉ 192 Main
Street, Proserpine ☎ (07) 4945 3711

🕐 Mon–Fri 9–5, Sat–Sun 9–3

a drive from Cairns to the Daintree

This extremely scenic drive takes you beyond the holiday city of Cairns via the coastline to charming Port Douglas and the Daintree's World Heritage-listed rainforest.

From central Cairns, take the Captain Cook Highway north out of town.

Stretching for 30km (18 miles), the beautiful Marlin Coast has many sandy beaches and small resort villages like Trinity Beach and Palm Cove. Other attractions along the way include Cairns Tropical Zoo and Hartley's Crocodile Adventures at Palm Cove, and the Rainforest Habitat near Port Douglas.

Continue on the highway, then take the Port Douglas turn-off.

Once a sleepy fishing settlement, charming Port Douglas is now a rather exclusive resort village, with high-quality accommodation, dining and shopping, a picturesque harbour and a perfect, long sandy beach.

Return to the highway and continue to Mossman.

Mossman has a sugar mill and a few other attractions, but this small town is essentially the gateway to the magnificent Daintree rainforest.

Take the Mossman Gorge Road.

This lush region, home to many orchid species, the large, flightless cassowary, birdwing butterflies and a rare tree kangaroo, was World Heritage-listed in 1988. The most easily accessible part of the Daintree National Park is Mossman Gorge, with a 2.7km (1.6-mile) circuit hiking trail.

After visiting the gorge, return to the main road to Daintree. Take the turn-off to the ferry.

Cross the Daintree River on the car ferry and you can take the bitumen (paved) road as far as Cape Tribulation (50km/31 miles). Several places off this road offer coastal tropical rainforests and white-sand beaches.

Return to Cairns via the same route.

Distance 320km (200 miles) **Time** One–two days, allowing for stops
Start/end point Central Cairns ✚ 10C
Lunch On the Inlet ($$) ✉ 3 Inlet Street, Port Douglas
☎ (07) 4099 5255

HOTELS

BRISBANE

Emporium Hotel ($$)

One of Brisbane's glitzier hotels, offering a pillow menu, rooftop pool, cocktail bar and restaurant. Five minutes from the CBD.

✉ 1000 Ann Street, Fortitude Valley ☎ (07) 3253 6999; www.emporiumhotel.com.au 🚉 Brunswick Street

M on Mary ($–$$$)

See page 68.

Stamford Plaza Brisbane ($$$)

Large and luxurious waterfront hotel, close to the Botanic Gardens.

✉ Corner of Edward and Margaret streets ☎ (07) 3221 1999; www.stamford.com.au 🚉 Central Station

CAIRNS

Hotel Sofitel Reef Casino Cairns ($$$)

Part of the Cairns casino complex, this hotel provides all the expected luxuries and a few more besides.

✉ 35–41 Wharf Street ☎ (07) 4030 8888; www.reefcasino.com.au 🚌 None

Reef Palms ($–$$)

See page 68.

GOLD COAST

Marriott Surfers Paradise Resort ($$–$$$)

A spacious hotel tower, with comfortable rooms, balconies, pools and small gym.

✉ Corner Surfers Paradise Boulevard and Hanlon Street, Surfers Paradise ☎ (07) 5579 3499, www.marriott.com 🚌 1A

SUNSHINE COAST

Netanya Noosa ($$$)

A delightful low-rise beachfront resort offering luxury suite accommodation.

✉ 75 Hastings Street, Noosa Heads ☎ (07) 5447 4722; www.netanyanoosa.com.au 🔲 None

RESTAURANTS

BRISBANE
Baguette ($$–$$$)
Renowned restaurant. French, Australian and Asian influences.
✉ 150 Racecourse Road, Ascot ☎ (07) 3268 6168; www.baguette.com.au
🕐 Lunch Mon–Fri, dinner Mon–Sat 🚌 300, 303

City Gardens Café ($–$$)
See page 61.

Pier Nine ($$–$$$)
An excellent riverside seafood restaurant.
✉ Eagle Street Pier, Brisbane ☎ (07) 3226 2100; www.piernine.com.au
🕐 Lunch Sat, dinner Mon–Sat 🚢 Riverside

TROPICAL NORTH QUEENSLAND
Nautilus ($$$)
Fine seafood is the speciality of this exclusive restaurant, set in a rainforest garden.
✉ 17 Murphy Street, Port Douglas ☎ (07) 4099 5330;
www.nautilus-restaurant.com.au 🕐 Dinner 🔲 None

SUNSHINE COAST
Ricky Ricardos ($$–$$$)
A long-standing popular restaurant with modern dishes in a riverside setting.
✉ Noosa Wharf, Quamby Place, Noosa Heads ☎ (07) 5447 2455 🕐 Lunch and dinner 🔲 None

The Spirit House ($$)
Although it's located inland from the coast, this superb Asian-style restaurant, in a unique rainforest setting, is well worth a visit.
✉ 20 Ninderry Road, Yandina ☎ (07) 5446 8994; www.spirithouse.com.au
🕐 Lunch daily, dinner Wed–Sat 🔲 None

SHOPPING

LOCAL ART AND DESIGN
Museum of Brisbane Store
Broad range of locally produced music, literature and souvenirs.
✉ Ground floor, Brisbane City Hall, King George Square ☎ (07) 3403 4355
🕐 Daily 10–5 🚇 Central Station

OPALS, GEMS AND JEWELLERY
Quilpie Opals
Leading opal specialist selling stones direct from the mines.
✉ Lennons Plaza, 68 Queen Street, Brisbane ☎ (07) 3221 7369 🚌 The Loop

SHOPPING CENTRES
Marina Mirage
A waterfront Gold Coast shopping centre with 80 speciality shops, boutiques and art galleries.
✉ 74 Seaworld Drive, Broadwater Spit, Main Beach, Gold Coast
☎ (07) 5555 6400 🚌 1, 1A

ENTERTAINMENT

NIGHTLIFE
Conrad Jupiters Casino
The brash Gold Coast is the perfect venue for this glitzy casino.
✉ Gold Coast Highway, Broadbeach, Gold Coast ☎ (07) 5592 8100;
www.conrad.com.au 🕐 Daily 🚌 1,1A

Family
The ever-popular Family has four levels, and the city's best DJs.
✉ 8 McLachlan Street, Fortitude Valley ☎ (07)3852 5000;
www.thefamily.com.au 🚇 Brunswick Street

Press Club
The city's trendiest café and bar, with live music and DJs.
✉ Corner of Brunswick and Ann streets, Fortitude Valley, Brisbane
☎ (07) 3852 4000 🕐 Daily 🚇 Brunswick Street

Victoria and Tasmania

Australia's most southerly states hold many surprises – a cooler climate (including winter snows) than many would expect, tranquil farmland, rugged peaks, and coastlines lashed by the wild waters of Bass Strait, which divides Victoria from Tasmania.

Victoria, separated from New South Wales by the country's longest river, the Murray, is small and densely populated by Australian standards. From the gracious capital, Melbourne, it is easy to reach attractions that vary from dramatic coastlines to the ski fields and peaks of the Great Dividing Range.

Melbourne

Hobart

The compact island state of Tasmania is packed with interest. Its violent convict past intrigues history lovers, while the superb coastal, mountain and wilderness scenery provides endless opportunities for outdoor activities. You can fly to Hobart and Launceston from the mainland, or take the *Spirit of Tasmania* ferry from Melbourne to Devonport.

www.visitvictoria.com
www.discovertasmania.com.au

MELBOURNE

Australia's second largest city, with a population of around 3.5 million, Melbourne is very different to its glossy northern sister. Founded almost 50 years after Sydney, in 1835, this more elegant, European-style city retains many grand buildings. Melburnians are known for their passion, equally lavished on sport and the arts. Melbourne is home to Australian Rules Football and a thriving arts scene played out in festivals and events year-round. The climate is often 'four seasons in a day' and can be very hot in summer. Melbourne's cooler winter temperatures are often accompanied by romantic, grey days.

Melbourne has much to recommend it to visitors: there are over 4,000 restaurants and the dining scene is superb; the shopping rivals that of Sydney; sport is practically a religion; and there is plenty of nightlife – including high-quality theatrical and cultural events and a world-class bar-scene.

A vibrant and dynamic city, bisected by the Yarra River, the central city area contains many museums and galleries, gracious avenues and charming laneways, and an abundance of green open spaces. Another Melbourne delight is riding the tram network; trams have practically disappeared from all other Australian cities, but in Melbourne this is very much the way to get around.

This is a city of many ethnic groups, as a visit to Chinatown and the Museum of Chinese Australian History, or the suburbs of Italian-influenced Carlton and multicultural Richmond reveal. Other enclaves are St Kilda (➤ 128–129) and South Yarra, with boutiques and the grand 1840s house, Como.

www.visitmelbourne.com

✚ 21K

Eureka Skydeck 88

The world's tallest residential tower, Eureka Tower, has Skydeck on its 88th floor, the southern hemisphere's highest viewing platform, at 285m (935ft). For added thrills there is the Edge – a glass cube

that projects 3m (almost 10ft) out of the building the same height as the viewing platform.

www.skydeck.com.au

✉ 7 Riverside Quay Southbank ☎ (03) 9693 8888 🕐 Daily 10–10, last entry 9:30 ✋ Moderate–expensive

Federation Square

The hub of town, Federation Square, is hard to miss. The city's main public gathering place hosts around 2,000 events each year, and sits alongside the riverside park called Birrarung Marr, from where bikes are hired and river cruises depart. Along with cafés, restaurants and bars, Fed Square is the address for many of the city's cultural institutions, including the Australian Centre for the Moving Image (ACMI), dedicated to screen culture; the National Gallery of Victoria's impressive Australian collection (NGV:A, the international collection, is a few hundred metres away at 180 St Kilda Road); the National Design Centre's gallery and retail space; and the Champions: Racing Museum & Hall of Fame, dedicated to horse racing.

www.federationsquare.com.au

✉ Corner Swanston and Flinders streets ☎ (03) 9655 1900 🚌 Flinders Street ❓ 1-hour guided tours Mon–Sat 11 and 2

Melbourne Cricket Ground & National Sports Museum

Visiting this most hallowed of Australia's sporting venues is a must – particularly on match days with the roar of 100,000 fans and the tension of a cricket test is palpable. Built in 1853, the first ever test was played here, as well as countless AFL games and grand finals. The MCG's Olympic Stand houses the National Sports Museum.

www.mcg.org.au; **www.**nsm.org.au

✉ Yarra Park, Jolimont ☎ (03) 9657 8879 ⏰ Daily 10–5, last entry at 4, except on event days. Closed Good Fri, 25 Dec ♿ Moderate 🍴 Coffee shop ($) 🚊 Trams 48, 75 ❓ Regular guided tours 10–3 on non-event days

Melbourne Museum
This modern complex is the largest museum in the southern hemisphere. Highlights include the Science and Life Gallery and the Bunjilaka Aboriginal Centre, a 'living forest' complete with wildlife, and an IMAX theatre.
www.melbourne.museum.vic.gov.au
✉ 11 Nicholson Street, Carlton ☎ 13 1102 🕑 Daily 10–5 ✋ Inexpensive
🚌 Trams 86, 96, City Circle

Old Melbourne Gaol

Although rather grim, this mid-19th century building is fascinating. The gaol, scene of 135 hangings – including that of the notorious bushranger Ned Kelly on 11 November 1880 – provides an idea of what colonial 19th-century prison life was like, and contains many intriguing exhibits, including death masks and a flogging triangle.
✉ Russell Street ☎ (03) 8663 7228 ⏰ Daily 9:30–5. Closed Good Fri and 25 Dec ✋ Moderate 🚋 City Circle tram ❓ Atmospheric evening tours available

St Kilda

Melbourne has many lively suburbs which provide a venue for Melburnians to let their hair down. Located on the shores of Port

Phillip Bay, St Kilda has been the city's seaside resort since the 1880s, when the pier was constructed. Its waterfront pathway is popular with walkers, cyclists and in-line skaters, and the Luna Park funfair, built in 1912, continues to be a great attraction. There are dozens of bustling cafés and restaurants, particularly on Acland Street. The Sunday arts and crafts markets are good, and you can take a cruise on the bay from the St Kilda Pier.

www.visitvictoria.com

🚋 Any St Kilda tram

ℹ Melbourne Visitor Information Centre ✉ Federation Square ☎ (03) 9658 9658 🕓 Daily 9–6

a walk around the Yarra River, Kings Domain and Botanic Gardens

This walk ventures beyond Melbourne's city centre, along the Yarra River and into the large area of parkland to the south.

Start at Flinders Street Station (corner of Swanston and Flinders streets), then cross Princes Bridge and turn right for Southbank Promenade.

There are many temptations here in the large Southgate shopping and eating complex. If you can, just admire the view of the city and river from the promenade, turn your back to Southbank and continue walking (east).

Walk under Princes Bridge and follow the path beside the river.

After walking along the Yarra, head away from the water at Swan Street Bridge and into the Kings Domain. This lush parkland encompasses impressive Government House, the official residence of the Governor of Victoria.

Continue into the gardens.

The delightful Royal Botanic Gardens are centred around an extensive ornamental lake. They contain some 60,000 plants and are one of central Melbourne's most attractive features.

Follow the signs to the Shrine of Remembrance.

The Shrine of Remembrance is an impressive landmark devoted to the servicemen and women of the various wars. Tours are at 11 and 2 daily, and depart from the Shrine visitors centre.

From here you can either cross St Kilda Road and take a tram to Flinders Street Station, or walk back via the Kings Domain and stop in at the National Gallery's international collection (180 St Kilda Road).

Distance 4 km (2.5 miles)
Time 2–4 hours, including time for a light lunch
Start/end point Flinders Street Station
🚋 Any tram along St Kilda Road
Lunch Observatory Café ($–$$) ✉ Royal Botanic Gardens ☎ (03) 9650 5600

More to see in Victoria

BALLARAT

Gold was discovered near Ballarat in 1851, an event that was to bring incredible wealth to the colony, and this elegant city

still contains many grand buildings from those days. The main attraction is the excellent **Sovereign Hill** historical park, a recreation of the gold-rush era. Other sights are the Ballarat Wildlife Park and Ballarat Fine Art Gallery.

www.visitballarat.com.au

➕ 21K

Sovereign Hill

✉ Bradshaw Street ☎ (03) 5337 1100; www.sovereignhill.com.au 🕐 Daily 10–5. Closed 25 Dec ✋ Expensive

DANDENONG RANGES

Just 40km (25 miles) east of Melbourne are the delightful Dandenong Ranges – cool, moist hills cloaked with eucalypts and rainforest. Their many attractions include Puffing Billy, a quaint steam train which runs between Belgrave and Gembrook, and the William Ricketts Sanctuary, an unusual park featuring Aboriginal-themed sculptures.

www.parkweb.vic.gov.au
www.visitvictoria.com

✚ 22K 🚉 Upper Ferntree Gully or Belgrave

ℹ Visitor Centre ✉ 1211 Burwood Highway, Upper Ferntree Gully ☎ 1800 645 505 or (03) 9758 7522 🕓 Daily 9–5. Closed Good Fri, 25 Dec

GREAT OCEAN ROAD
Best places to see, ➤ 44–45.

PHILLIP ISLAND
This scenic island, linked by bridge to the mainland, is famous for
its nightly Penguin Parade – tiny fairy penguins waddling ashore to

their burrows. The site of the parade and its visitor centre at Summerland Beach are part of the **Phillip Island Nature Park,** which incorporates the island's Koala Conservation Centre (near the main town of Cowes), the ideal place to meet these cuddly marsupials.

www.visitphillipisland.com; **www.**penguins.org.au

✚ 21L

🛈 Visitor Information Centre
✉ 895 Phillip Island Tourist Road, Newhaven ☎ 1300 366 422 or (03) 5956 7447 🕓 Daily 9–5
Phillip Island Nature Park
☎ (03) 5951 2800 🕓 Koala Centre: daily 10–5:30. Penguin Centre: daily from 10am 💷 Moderate–expensive
🚌 From Melbourne

WILSONS PROMONTORY NATIONAL PARK

The spectacular 'Prom' forms the Australian mainland's most southerly point. This is one of Victoria's most popular national parks, offering beaches and superb coastal scenery, rainforests, well-marked hiking trails, and a wide range of flora and fauna.

www.parkweb.vic.gov.au
✚ 22L 💷 Inexpensive
🛈 Visitor Centre ✉ Tidal River
☎ (03) 5680 9555 🕓 Daily from 8:30am ❓ Bookings required for campsites during peak times

Tasmania
HOBART

Tasmania's capital is one of Australia's most pleasant settlements. Hobart, on the River Derwent, is full of old colonial buildings; walking is the best way to appreciate the historic atmosphere. While here, take a river cruise and a trip to Mount Wellington (1,270m/4,167ft), which dominates the city – the view is sensational.

www.hobarttravelcentre.com.au

✚ 22M

Battery Point

With its charming mid-19th-century cottages and

houses, craft and antiques shops and quaint streets like Arthur's Circus, this inner city 'village' is Hobart's showpiece. Highlights are the Narryna Heritage Museum's collection of 19th-century items and the 1818 Signal Station and military base from which the suburb takes its name.

Narryna Heritage Museum

✉ 103 Hampden Road ☎ (03) 6234 2791 🕙 Tue–Fri 10:30–5, Sat–Sun 2–5. Closed Good Fri, Anzac Day, 25 Dec and Jul 👋 Inexpensive

Mount Wellington

Hobart's dramatic backdrop, Mount Wellington, makes a great trip, and is a 20-minute drive from the centre of town. The ascent to the summit leads through temperate rainforest and sub-alpine landscapes marked by towering dolerite columns. From the summit, the views over the city are stunning, weather permitting. There are a number of bushwalking trails, of varying lengths and difficulty, leading off from points along the access road.

www.wellingtonpark.tas.gov.au

🚌 Private shuttle from the visitors centre daily at 9:30 and 1:30

Salamanca Place
This delightful old dockside street is lined with sandstone warehouses converted into restaurants and arts and crafts shops, and is the venue for Hobart's lively Salamanca market on Saturdays (► 77). The Salamanca Arts Centre is along here, and well worth a visit, with shops, galleries and performances.
www.discovertasmania.com.au
✉ Salamanca Place ⚫ Market: Sat 8:30–3 ✋ Free 🍴 Many cafés and restaurants ($–$$$)

Tasmanian Museum And Art Gallery
Hobart's Tasmanian Museum contains some fine and varied exhibits, particularly on Australian mammals, convict history, the indigenous Tasmanians and Tasmania's close links with Antarctica. The attached art gallery holds a good collection of colonial art. An ideal place to discover the island's history.
www.tmag.tas.gov.au
✉ 40 Macquarie Street ☎ (03) 6211 4177 ⚫ Daily 10–5. Closed Good Fri, 25 Apr and 25 Dec ✋ Free

More to see in Tasmania

FREYCINET PENINSULA
Tasmania's east coast is renowned for beautiful scenery, none of which surpasses that of **Freycinet National Park** with its sandy white beaches, granite peaks and abundance of plants, birds and animals. The park is reached via the fishing settlement of Coles Bay. The town of Bicheno has more lovely beaches, great diving and a wildlife park.
www.freycinetcolesbay.com
➕ 22M 🚌 Tassie Link from Hobart ℹ Visitor Centre ✉ Freycinet Drive, Freycinet National Park ☎ (03) 6256 7000 ⚫ Daily 8–6; winter 8–5

LAUNCESTON

Tasmania's second city, situated on the Tamar River and founded in 1805 (a year after Hobart), has retained many of its old buildings, which can be viewed on a self-guided walk around town. There are pleasant parks and reserves – a visit to the spectacular Cataract Gorge Reserve is recommended. The Queen Victoria Museum and Art Gallery, located at two sites (city centre and across the river at Inveresk) is also worth a visit. The Launceston region is rich in historic houses and wineries.

www.discovertasmania.com.au

 22L  or  Launceston
 Information Centre ✉ 12–16 St John Street ☎ (03) 6336 3133
🕐 Mon–Fri 9–5, Sat 9–3, Sun 9–12

THE MIDLANDS

The Midlands Highway, running for 200km (124 miles) between
Hobart and Launceston, passes through charming and historic
towns. Oatlands is full of atmospheric old buildings such as the
Court House, while, further north, picturesque Ross is famous
for its 1836 bridge and contains the **Tasmanian Wool Centre,**
devoted to the state's extensive wool industry.
 22M

Tasmanian Wool Centre
✉ Church Street, Ross ☎ (03) 6381 5466; www.taswoolcentre.com.au
🕐 Daily 9–5 🖐 Inexpensive 🚌 Tasmanian Redline from Hobart

141

PORT ARTHUR AND THE TASMAN PENINSULA

Established in 1830 as a far-flung penal settlement for the worst convict offenders, Port Arthur has over 30 ruins and historic sites, an excellent museum, and the settlement's poignant burial ground, the Isle of the Dead.

The surrounding Tasman Peninsula has magnificent scenery on the east coast and the Tasmanian Devil Park with an excellent wildlife collection.

www.portarthur.org.au

➕ 22M ✉ Port Arthur Historic Site ☎ 1800 659 101 or (03) 6251 2300 🕒 Daily 8:30–dusk

✋ Expensive; includes cruise and guided walk 🚌 Tassie Link from Hobart

STRAHAN

The lightly populated west coast is a region of wild coastline, rivers and forest lands. From the waterside village of Strahan (pronounced 'Strawn') you can go fishing, take the West Coast Wilderness Railway, and cruise Macquarie Harbour – once the site of the brutal Sarah Island penal settlement – and the pristine Gordon River, part of the World Heritage-listed Franklin-Gordon Wild Rivers National Park. In town, the **Strahan Visitor Centre** provides a fascinating lesson in local history.

➕ 21M

Strahan Visitor Centre

✉ The Esplanade ☎ (03) 6472 6800; www.tasmaniawestcoast.com.au

🕒 Daily 10–6 ✋ Inexpensive 🚌 Tassie Link to Strahan

TASMANIA'S WORLD HERITAGE AREA

Best places to see, ➤ 52–53.

HOTELS

VICTORIA
MELBOURNE
The Langham ($$$)
See page 69.

Novotel St Kilda ($$)
A large hotel on Port Phillip Bay with a spa, heated pool and gym.
✉ 16 The Esplanade, St Kilda ☎ (03) 9525 5522;
www.novotelstkilda.com.au 🚋 Any St Kilda tram

Victoria Hotel ($–$$)
See page 69.

TASMANIA
HOBART
Mercure Hotel Hobart ($–$$)
Centrally located, good-value hotel with pleasant rooms.
✉ 156 Bathurst Street ☎ (03) 6232 6255; www.accorhotels.com.au

Somerset on the Pier ($$$)
See page 69.

RESTAURANTS

VICTORIA
MELBOURNE
Stokehouse ($-$$$)
The beachfront Stokehouse is a much celebrated establishment,
with fine dining upstairs and casual fare downstairs.
✉ 30 Jacka Boulevard, St Kilda ☎ (03) 9525 5555 🕐 Lunch and dinner
daily 🚋 Any St Kilda tram.

Taxi Dining Room ($$$)
Innovative dining, a hybrid of Japanese/Euro/Mod-Oz, in snazzy
surrounds with great views.
✉ Transport Hotel, Federation Square, corner Swanston and Flinders streets
☎ (03) 9654 8801; reservations required 🚉 Flinders Street Station

Journal Canteen ($)
See page 61.

BALLARAT
Tozers at the Ansonia ($$)
Excellent Modern Australian cuisine in a smart boutique hotel.
✉ 32 Lydiard Street South ☎ (03) 5332 4678 🕓 Lunch Tue–Fri, dinner
Mon–Sat

GREAT OCEAN ROAD
Chris's Restaurant ($$–$$$)
Inventive seafood and Greek-influenced meals with an ocean view.
✉ 280 Skenes Creek Road, Apollo Bay ☎ (03) 5237 6411 🕓 Breakfast, lunch
and dinner daily

Merrijig Inn ($$–$$$)
Cutting-edge Mediterranean fare in a cosy and elegant dining
room.
✉ 1 Campbell Street, Port Fairy ☎ (03) 5568 2324 🕓 Dinner Mon–Sat

DANDENONG RANGES
Woods ($$)
Asian-fusion menu emphasizing organic and free-range
ingredients.
✉ 21 Sherbrooke Road, Sherbrooke ☎ (03) 9755 2131 🕓 Breakfast, lunch
and dinner Fri–Sun

TASMANIA
HOBART
Alexanders Restaurant ($$$)
Fine dining in a colonial mansion, with a menu that makes the
most of local ingredients.
✉ Corner Salamanca Place and Runnymede Street, Battery Point ☎ (03)
6232 3900 🕓 Dinner daily

Annapurna ($–$$)

Inexpensive, excellent Indian food and good vegetarian options.

✉ 93 Salamanca Place, Hobart ☎ (03) 6224 0400;
www.annapurnaindiancuisine.com 🕐 Lunch Wed–Sun, dinner daily

Mures Upper Deck ($$–$$$)

See page 61.

Retro Café ($)

Serving perfect coffee and casual café fare here on the waterfront
for over a decade.

✉ 31 Salamanca Place ☎ (03) 6223 3073 🕐 Breakfast and lunch

DEVONPORT
Essence Food & Wine ($–$$)

Contemporary Australian fare in a renovated cottage, with a
separate lounge-bar.

✉ 28 Forbes Street ☎ (03) 6424 6431 🕐 Lunch Wed and Fri, dinner
Tue–Sat

LAUNCESTON
Fee and Me ($$–$$$)

Putting an Australian spin on Spanish-style dining, Fee and Me's
menu presents Mod-Oz entrée-sized dishes (three to five
suggested per person).

✉ 190 Charles Street ☎ (03) 6331 3195; www.feeandme.com.au 🕐 Dinner
Tue–Sat

Star Hotel ($–$$)

Offering great pub-grub – like wood-fired pizza, pasta and tapas –
the Star is popular for its live entertainment weekends.

✉ 113 Charles Street ☎ (03) 6331 6111 🕐 Lunch and dinner daily

PORT ARTHUR
Felons Restaurant ($$)

Creates innovative dishes from the best local produce.

✉ Visitor Centre, Port Arthur Historic Site ☎ (03) 6251 2310 🕐 Dinner daily

SHOPPING

AUSTRALIANA
Counter
See page 73.

Chapel Street
Great shopping with boutiques stretching through South Yarra and Prahan in the inner-city.
✉ South Yarra and Prahran, Melbourne 🚋 Trams 6, 8, 72

Naturally Tasmanian
See page 73.

ABORIGINAL ARTS
Koorie Heritage Trust
See page 72.

CRAFT AND DESIGN
eg.etal
A leading commercial gallery-store for Australia's jewellery designers.
✉ 185 Little Collins Street, Melbourne ☎ (03) 9663 4334 🚋 None

ENTERTAINMENT

Half-Tix
Half-price tickets for theatre, dance, comedy and music shows on the day of performance. Cash purchases only.
✉ Melbourne Town Hall, 120 Swanston Street, Melbourne; www.halftixmelbourne.com 🕐 Mon 10–2, Tue–Thu 11–6, Fri 11–6:30, Sat 10–4

The Toff
Catch artsy live acts, DJs, drinks or even dinner at this eclectic venue.
✉ Second Floor, Curtin House, 252 Swanston Street, Melbourne ☎ (03) 9639 8770, www.thetoffintown.com 🕐 Tue–Sun

South Australia and the Northern Territory

These two vastly different regions combined comprise the middle of Australia. Historically, they were joined politically with the South Australian government acquiring the 1.3 million sq km (501,800sq miles) to the north in 1863, which it shed in 1911 – perceived, as it was, as untameable.

South Australia was settled in 1836 by non-convicts. Its relatively small area covers fertile farming and wine-producing regions, outside the capital Adelaide. The arid Outback infiltrates much of the state. The enormous and sparsely populated Northern Territory combines the desert lands of the 'Red Centre' with the 'tropical top-end'.

Its significant Aboriginal population co-manages many of the Northern Territory's major attractions, like Kakadu and Uluru. The 2,979km (1,851 miles) between Adelaide and Darwin is connected by the famous Ghan train.
www.southaustralia.com
www.travelnt.com

147

ADELAIDE

South Australia's capital was first settled in December 1836, when HMS *Buffalo* docked at Glenelg with her 'cargo' of free settlers. Unlike many Australian cities, Adelaide was planned – Englishman Colonel William Light was responsible for the grid of city-centre streets. Adelaide was once known as the 'City of Churches' and for its conservative citizens, but today the 1.1 million population enjoys an enviable lifestyle and a Mediterranean climate.

Surrounded by large areas of parkland and the Adelaide Hills, the compact city centre is a delightful place to explore; there are many old buildings, relatively little traffic, and a sense of calm which is rare in urban environments. This elegant city is famous for its café and restaurant scene, as well as a thriving artistic and cultural life. The ideal time to be here is during the biennial (every even-numbered year), internationally acclaimed Adelaide Festival of Arts, when the city comes alive with everything from classical music concerts to outrageous fringe theatre.

In addition to visiting the museums and attractions detailed below, you should take a cruise on the placid and scenic River Torrens, which passes through the city. Within the metropolitan area, you can also visit the seaside suburb of Glenelg, where the first settlers landed in 1836 – it can be reached by a tram ride from the city centre. The historic settlement of Port Adelaide was once the city's harbour town, but now concentrates on its heritage attractions, including the South Australian Maritime Museum and the National Railway Museum complex, the largest of its kind in the country.

www.adelaide.southaustralia.com

 20K

Art Gallery of South Australia and North Terrace

A stroll down North Terrace, Adelaide's grandest
avenue, is the best way to see the city's historic
buildings, several of which are open to the public. At
the western end are the Adelaide Casino, in a restored
1920s railway station, Old Parliament House, and the
latter's neighbouring, much more impressive
successor. East of King William Street lie the South
Australian Museum (➤ 151); the Art Gallery of South
Australia, with around 35,000 works, including a
significant Australian collection; and the 1840s Ayers
House – former home of Sir Henry Ayers, who was
seven times premier of South Australia.

www.artgallery.sa.gov.au

✉ Art Gallery of South Australia: North Terrace ☎ (08) 8207
7000 🕐 Daily 10–5. Closed 25 Dec 🎟 Free general admission
🍽 Art Gallery Café ($–$$) 🚌 City Loop ❓ Free guided tours
at 11 and 2

Glenelg

Take the vintage tram from Victoria Square in the city to this popular seaside suburb. Just 10km (6 miles) from Adelaide, Glenelg is steeped in colonial history, with markers and structures dating back to 1836. The long sandy beach and jetty, backed by high-rise buildings, are lined with beachgoers. There's a waterpark and a carnival atmosphere in summer, and plenty of cafés and restaurants.

✉ Glenelg Visitor Centre, Foreshore ☎ (08) 8294 5833 🕐 Mon–Fri 9–5, Sat–Sun 10–3 ✋ Free 🚌 Glenelg tram or 138 bus

South Australian Museum

The highlights of this better-than-average museum include its internationally acclaimed Australian Aboriginal exhibit, with over 3,000 items on display, and Pacfic Cultures gallery – the largest in Australia. And, of course, there are the usual natural history and general ethnographic and anthropological displays. Free guided tours daily.

www.samuseum.sa.gov.au

✉ North Terrace ☎ (08) 8207 7500 🕐 Daily 10–5. Closed Good Fri, 25 Dec ✋ Free 🚌 City Loop

Tandanya National Aboriginal Cultural Institute

This illuminating Aboriginal centre is one of a few of its kind in Australia. Including galleries with high-quality changing art exhibitions, workshops, and an area for dance and other performing arts, Tandanya (the local Aboriginal name for the Adelaide region) is a must for visitors. The centre has a shop selling authentic gifts, such as paintings and baskets, sourced directly from artists.

www.tandanya.com.au

✉ 253 Grenfell Street ☎ (08) 8224 3200 🕐 Daily 10–5 ✋ Inexpensive 🚌 City Loop

a walk around North Adelaide and the City Parklands

An easy walk which takes you beyond the city centre and into some of Adelaide's delightful parklands.

Start on King William Road, just beyond the junction with North Terrace.

The Adelaide Festival Centre is the heart of Adelaide's arts scene. The large modern building houses several performance halls and a performing arts museum. River cruises start in front of the centre.

Continue north on King William Road, crossing the River Torrens on Adelaide Bridge.

St Peter's Cathedral dates from 1869; the bells are the heaviest and finest in the southern hemisphere.

Walk along Pennington Terrace to reach Montefiore Hill.

From the lookout, 'Light's Vision', next to the statue of Colonel William Light, there are wonderful views.

Walk up Jeffcott Street towards Wellington Square, then turn right at Archer Street to reach O'Connell Street.

The elegant suburb of North Adelaide contains many grand old homes. A lively pub, café and gallery scene thrives along O'Connell and Melbourne streets.

From O'Connell Street, turn left into Brougham Place, then right into Frome Road to reach Melbourne Street. Return to Frome Road and cross the River Torrens via Albert Bridge to Adelaide's small zoo.

Australia's oldest zoo has aviaries, a reptile house and an entertaining collection of Australian mammals.

Follow the signs to the Botanic Garden.

Don't miss the garden's Bicentennial Conservatory, a vast, glass dome containing a tropical rainforest; or the nearby National Wine Centre.

Return to North Terrace.

Distance 4km (2.5 miles)
Time 2–4 hours, depending on time at the zoo and in the gardens
Start point Adelaide Festival Centre 🚌 City Loop
End point North Terrace 🚌 City Loop
Lunch The Oxford Hotel (➤ 169)

More to see in South Australia

ADELAIDE HILLS

Around 20 minutes east of the city, this region of hills, bushland, vineyards and picturesque small towns is a popular weekend destination. Attractions include good views from the summit of Mount Lofty, botanic gardens, the acclaimed National Motor Museum at Birdwood, and Warrawong Wildlife Sanctuary – an important wildlife reserve. The German-style main town of Hahndorf has fine artworks in the Hahndorf Academy.

www.visitadelaidehills.com.au

🚆 20K 🚌 From Adelaide

ℹ️ Visitor Information Centre ✉️ 41 Main Street, Hahndorf ☎️ (08) 8388 1185

🕐 Mon–Fri 9–5, Sat–Sun 10–4

BAROSSA VALLEY

The renowned wine-producing area of the Barossa was settled in the 1830s by Silesians and Prussians, and this picturesque valley is characterized by distinctive European architecture, traditions and cuisine. You can visit some of the 50 or so wineries, and enjoy the ambience of towns and villages like Tanunda, Bethany, Lyndoch and Angaston.

www.barossa.com

✚ 20K 🚌 From Adelaide

ℹ️ Barossa Visitor Information Centre ✉️ 66–68 Murray Street, Tanunda
☎️ 1300 852 982 or (08) 8563 0600 🕐 Mon–Fri 9–5, Sat–Sun 10–4. Closed Good Fri, 25 Dec

FLINDERS RANGES NATIONAL PARK

A rugged desert mountain chain containing one of the most ancient landscapes on earth. Plenty of wildlife can be found, while there are several good hikes that allow you to see the diverse plantlife. The highlights of the park are Wilpena Pound, an enormous 80sq km (30sq-mile) elevated amphitheatre surrounded by sheer cliffs, and St Mary's Peak (1,171m/3,842ft), a challenging walk for experienced hikers. The area is rich in Aboriginal art.

www.environment.sa.gov.au

🚩 20J 🖐 Inexpensive 🚌 or ✖ From Adelaide 🛈 Wilpena Pound Visitor Centre ☎ (08) 8648 0048 🕐 Daily 8–6

KANGAROO ISLAND

Australia's third largest island is a relaxed place with spectacular scenery, remarkable wildlife and pleasant small towns like the main settlement of Kingscote. There are rugged cliffs and sandy beaches; a large part of the island is within Flinders Chase National Park, domain of kangaroos, koalas and prolific birdlife; and you can view Australian sea lions from close quarters at Seal Bay Conservation Park.

www.tourkangarooisland.com.au

⊞ 19K ⊠ From Adelaide
🚢 From Cape Jervis
ℹ️ Kangaroo Island Gateway Visitor Centre
✉️ Howard Drive, Penneshaw ☎ 1800 811 080 or (08) 8553 1185 🕐 Mon–Fri 9–5, Sat–Sun 10–4. Closed 25 Dec

DARWIN

The Northern Territory's capital and largest city was founded in 1869. Situated closer to Asia than to any major Australian cities, it has a multicultural population of about 108,000. Darwin was bombed by the Japanese during World War II, and suffered another catastrophe in 1974, when Cyclone Tracy virtually flattened the city. Located on vast Darwin Harbour (on which a cruise is highly recommended), this tropical, modern settlement is a laid-back place. A few reminders of Darwin's history remain: you can visit the 1883 Fannie Bay Gaol and take a historical walk around the city centre.

www.travelnt.com ✚ 6B

Darwin Wharf Precinct

The wharf precinct's recent major redevelopment added a public wave pool and convention centre in 2008, plus hotels and apartment towers in 2009, reinvigorating Darwin's waterfront.

The old Stokes Wharf is good for a wander around dinnertime when the arcade's many fish-and-chip booths get going. And the nearby Deckchair Cinema (Apr–Nov) is an outdoor movie theatre.

www.waterfront.nt.gov.au

✉ Stokes Hill Wharf ☎ (08) 8981 4268 ⏱ Precinct: daily

George Brown Darwin Botanic Gardens
Containing the southern hemisphere's most extensive collection of tropical palms, orchids, a rainforest area and wetlands flora, Darwin's gardens are a delightful place in which to relax or escape the heat.

✉ Geranium Street ☎ (08) 8981 1958 🕐 Daily 7–7 👆 Free

Mindil Beach
Although swimming is not recommended due to box jellyfish, sharks and crocodiles, this pleasant beach offers a park, wonderful sunsets, Darwin's casino and the famous **Mindil Beach Sunset Markets** (► 77).

Mindil Beach Sunset Markets
🕐 May–Oct Thu 5–10, Sun 4–9

Museum and Art Gallery of The Northern Territory
This well-planned, modern complex includes the Maritime Museum, a good collection of Aboriginal and Australian art, and displays on local and military history, natural science and Cyclone Tracy (➤ 158). There is a good café and retail outlet here.
www.magnt.nt.gov.au
✉ Conacher Street, Bullocky Point ☎ (00) 8999 8264 🕐 Mon–Fri 9–5, Sat–Sun 10–5. Closed Good Fri, 25 and 26 Dec, 1 Jan ✋ Free

More to see in the Northern Territory

ALICE SPRINGS

Affectionately known as 'The Alice', this unpretentious Outback town at the heart of the continent was founded as a remote Overland Telegraph station in 1871. Alice Springs is full of attractions: you can take a camel ride, or visit the Old Telegraph Station, the Royal Flying Doctor Service base and the fascinating Cultural Precinct, with an arts centre, cemetery, sculpture garden and natural history collection.

Nearby, the rugged MacDonnell Ranges contain steep gorges, nature reserves, historic settlements and homesteads, ancient Aboriginal sites, national parks and safe swimming waterholes.
www.centralaustraliantourism.com

✚ 7E 🚆 The Ghan from Darwin, Adelaide and Sydney ✈ Alice Springs
ℹ Central Australian Tourism Industry Association ✉ 60 Gregory Terrace
☎ 1800 645 199 or (08) 8952 5800 🕐 Mon–Fri 8:30–5:30, Sat–Sun 9–4

KAKADU NATIONAL PARK

Best places to see, ➤ 46–47.

KATHERINE AND NITMILUK NATIONAL PARK

Katherine, the Territory's third largest settlement, is a pleasant town with a museum, a nature reserve and some historic buildings. The main attraction is nearby Nitmiluk (Katherine Gorge) National Park, with 13 dramatic sandstone gorges. The best way to appreciate Nitmiluk is by hiking along sections of the extensive network of trails, or by taking a cruise on the Katherine River.
www.visitKatherine.com.au, www.nitmiluKtours.com.au

✚ 6B 🚌 Darwin and Alice Springs ✈ Katherine
ℹ Katherine Region Tourist Association ✉ Corner Lindsay Street and Katherine Terrace ☎ 1800 653 142 or (08) 8972 2650 🕐 Mon–Fri 8:30–5, Sat–Sun 8:30–4

TIWI ISLANDS

Melville and Bathurst islands, 80km (50 miles) north of Darwin, are known collectively as the Tiwis. They are home to the Tiwi Aboriginal people, celebrated for their unique art style, which includes ornately painted *pukumani* (burial) poles, screen printing and pottery. The Tiwis can be visited by tour only, which takes in the main Island, Nguiu, and its museum, church, cemetery and two arts centres.

➕ 6B ✈ or 🚢 From Darwin ✋ Expensive

ULURU–KATA TJUTA NATIONAL PARK

Best places to see, ➤ 54–55.

WATARRKA NATIONAL PARK

This remote, rugged desert park, north of Uluru, is famous for Kings Canyon – a spectacular sandstone gorge with walls over 300m (990ft) high. Visitors can explore lush waterholes and the strangely weathered rocks of the Lost City, and take a challenging bushwalk. There is a wide variety of flora and fauna, including some extraordinary ancient palm trees.

www.gov.au/nreta/parks/find/watarrka.html

➕ 6E ✋ Free 🚌 Tour
ℹ Central Australian Tourism Association
✉ 60 Gregory Terrace, Alice Springs ☎ 1800 645 199 or (08) 8952 5800

from Darwin to Litchfield National Park

This drive makes an easy day trip and takes in several attractions outside Darwin, plus a superb national park.

From Darwin's centre, follow the signs to the Stuart Highway and Winnellie.

In the outer suburb of Winnellie, the Australian Aviation Heritage Centre has a good collection of aircraft, including a massive B-52 bomber.

Continue south on the Highway.

Darwin Crocodile Farm, 40km (25 miles) south of Darwin, has over 36,000 saltwater and freshwater crocodiles. The farm, which breeds animals for their meat and skins, has a tourist facility.

Continue south, then take the Berry Springs turn-off.

Berry Springs has two major attractions – the large Territory Wildlife Park, with its excellent collection of native fauna, and the nearby Berry Springs Nature Park, a great spot for a swim or a barbecue.

Return to the Stuart Highway and drive south. Take the Batchelor turn-off.

The small settlement of Batchelor, once a dormitory town for workers at the nearby Rum Jungle uranium mine, is best known as the gateway to Litchfield National Park.

Continue for another 21km (13 miles) into the park.

Litchfield National Park, a rugged yet delightful reserve, was little known before the mid-1980s, as it was on private land. Today, visitors come here to enjoy the spectacular waterfalls, refreshing swimming holes, hiking trails and superb views of the region. Other highlights include a small 1930s pioneers' homestead; tall 'magnetic' termite mounds, so called because they always face north–south; and the Lost City, an area of curious sandstone pillars.

Return to Darwin via Batchelor and the Stuart Highway.

Distance 280km (174 miles)
Time A full day at least
Start/end point Central Darwin ✚ 6B
Lunch Territory Wildlife Park ($)
✉ Cox Peninsula Road, Berry Springs
☎ (08) 8988 7200;
www.territorywildlifepark.com.au

HOTELS

SOUTH AUSTRALIA
ADELAIDE
Hyatt Regency Adelaide ($$$)
Adelaide's finest hotel, right in the heart of the city.
✉ North Terrace ☎ (08) 8231 1234 🚌 City Loop or 99B

Quest Mansions ($–$$)
See page 69.

BAROSSA VALLEY
Novotel Barossa Valley Resort ($$–$$$)
Large resort with fitness facilities and an 18-hole golf course.
✉ Golf Links Road, Rowland Flat ☎ (08) 8524 0000;
www.novotelbarossa.com.au 🚌 From Adelaide

NORTHERN TERRITORY
DARWIN
Novotel Darwin Atrium $$
See page 69.

Quest Darwin ($$–$$$)
A range of slick self-contained apartments, from studio to two-bedroom.
✉ 55 Cavenagh Street ☎ (08) 8982 3100; www.questdarwin.com.au

RESTAURANTS

SOUTH AUSTRALIA
ADELAIDE
Botanic Cafe ($$)
Innovative Modern Italian menu, good wine list and great views.
✉ 4 East Terrace ☎ (08) 8232 0626 🕐 Lunch Mon–Fri, dinner Mon–Sat
🚌 City Loop

Jolleys Boathouse ($$)
See page 61.

North ($–$$)

Modern Australian menu and South Australian wines.

✉ Skycity, North Terrace, Adelaide ☎ (08) 8218 4273;
www.skycityadelaide.com.au 🕐 Lunch and dinner daily 🚌 99B, 99C

The Oxford Hotel ($$)

A long-running pub restaurant, serving Modern Australian dishes
that are deservedly popular with the locals.

✉ 101 O'Connell Street, North Adelaide ☎ (08) 8267 2652 🕐 Lunch
Mon–Fri, dinner Mon–Sat 🚌 182, 222

BAROSSA VALLEY
1918 Bistro and Grill ($$)

A rustic restaurant serving delicious Mod-Oz food.

✉ 94 Murray Street, Tanunda ☎ (08) 8563 0405; www.1918.com.au
🕐 Mon–Sat lunch and dinner daily 🚌 4, 6

NORTHERN TERRITORY
DARWIN
Cornucopia Museum Café ($$)

Waterfront café in Darwin's premier museum. Good-value meals.

✉ Conacher Street, Bullocky Point ☎ (08) 8981 1002;
www.cornucopiadarwin.com.au 🕐 Brunch and lunch daily 🚌 None

Hanuman ($$–$$$)

Quality Thai and Nonya (Malaysian) cuisine in the Holiday Inn hotel.

✉ 93 Mitchell Street ☎ (08) 8941 3500; www.hanuman.com.au 🕐 Lunch
Mon–Fri, dinner daily

ALICE SPRINGS
Bluegrass Restaurant ($$)

A wide variety of dishes, from kangaroo to vegetarian meals.

✉ Corner of Todd Street and Stott Terrace ☎ (08) 8955 5188;
www.bluegrassrestaurant.com.au 🕐 Lunch and dinner Wed–Mon

SHOPPING

ABORIGINAL ART
Framed
Aboriginal and non-Aboriginal art, crafts, sculptures and gifts.
✉ 55 Stuart Highway, Stuart Park, Darwin ☎ (08) 8981 2994 🖳 None

Papunya Tula Artists
See page 73.

OPALS, GEMS AND JEWELLERY
Olympic Opal Gem Mine
✉ 5 Rundle Mall, Adelaide ☎ (08) 8211 7440 🖳 City Loop

Paspaley Pearls
Northern Australian pearls – regarded as the world's finest – and other exquisite jewellery are sold here.
✉ 19 The Mall, Darwin ☎ (08) 8982 5555

ENTERTAINMENT

Adelaide Festival Centre
This modern complex is Adelaide's premier performing-arts venue.
✉ King William Road, Adelaide ☎ Box office: 13 12 46 🖳 City Loop

Skycity Adelaide
A casino within the grand 1920s Adelaide railway station.
✉ North Terrace, Adelaide ☎ (08) 8212 2811; www.skycityadelaide.com.au
🕐 Daily from 10am; closed Good Fri, 25 Dec 🖳 City Loop

Darwin Entertainment Centre
A large complex: Darwin's main concert, dance and theatre venue.
✉ 93 Mitchell Street, Darwin ☎ (08) 8980 3333;
www.darwinentertainment.com.au

Skycity Darwin
Beachfront casino complex and popular nightlife venue.
✉ Gilruth Avenue, Mindil Beach, Darwin ☎ (08) 8943 8888;
www.skycitydarwin.com.au 🕐 Daily

Western Australia

Western Australia takes up almost a third of the continent, but is home to just over 2 million people, the vast majority living in Perth and Fremantle. Much of the terrain is arid and used for cattle farming and mining. The discovery of gold in the southeast in the 1890s initially brought prosperity, and modern Western Australia has boomed because of the extraordinary wealth created by iron ore mining in particular.

Perth

Natural wonders here are remarkable: tall forests in the southwest; a coastline of white sandy beaches and rugged cliffs; extraordinary wildlife, including marsupials like the numbat and quokka, unique to the state; and the dramatic rock formations of the Kimberley in the far north. Many of the southern wild flowers are found nowhere else in Australia. There is much to see but distances are vast – flying is the best option for getting around.

www.westernaustralia.com

PERTH

Founded in 1829 by free settlers, and initially known as the Swan River Colony, Perth began life as an incredibly isolated outpost of Sydney and the eastern part of the continent. This isolation continues today. Despite its prosperity and cosmopolitan ambience, Perth is the world's most remote city – separated from the east by the desert lands of the Nullarbor Plain, with the nearest large centre, Adelaide, over 2,700km (1,680 miles) away. Much of Perth's charm is due to its location. The city is in a delightful setting on the broad Swan River; some of Australia's best urban beaches lie to the west; and the metropolitan area is backed by the low hills of the Darling Range to the east. The climate is warm and sunny, the generally rather affluent lifestyle is enviable, and the atmosphere is very relaxed for a state capital.

Perth's small modern city centre, much of which was reconstructed during the 1980s with the proceeds of the state's mineral wealth, offers quite a few attractions of its own. There are many historic buildings along St George's Terrace, many parks and gardens, excellent restaurants and some good nightlife venues. But the true delights of this western capital lie a little beyond the city centre.

Perth is seen at its best from the white sandy beaches of Cottesloo and Scarborough, and on cruises up the Swan River to the vineyards of the fertile Avon Valley. Another highlight is the ferry trip to the atmospheric port town of Fremantle (➤ 176), 19km (12 miles) downstream.

www.wavisitorcentre.com ✚ 13J

Kings Park

Overlooking the city and the Swan River, this popular 400ha (990-acre) reserve consists largely of unspoiled bushland, with colourful wild flowers and prolific birdlife. It also includes the Western Australian Botanic Garden and the State War Memorial and is the venue for regular events, festivals and guided walks.
www.bgpa.wa.gov.au

✉ Off Fraser Avenue ☎ (08) 9480 3600 ⏱ Daily ✋ Free ❚❚ Restaurants ($–$$) 🚌 33 or Perth Tram ❓ Free guided walks daily at 10 and 2

Perth Cultural Centre

A pedestrian thoroughfare, just north of the train station, links the city's main cultural institutions. The Centre incorporates the **Western Australian Museum**, with displays relating to Perth's maritime connections, Fremantle's history and the region's natural history.

The **Art Gallery of Western Australia** has an awesome collection of works by West Australians, including contemporary and traditional Aboriginal work. It also displays a formidable Australian art collection.

The **Perth Institute of Contemporary Arts (PICA)** has cutting-edge new works covered, including screen, performance and multimedia.

✉ James Street, Northbridge

✋ Free 🚆 Perth

Western Australian Museum:

☎ (08) 9212 3700;

www.musem.wa.gov.au

🕐 Daily 9:30–5. Closed Good Friday and 25 Dec

Art Gallery of Western Australia:

☎ (08) 9492 6600;

www.artgallery.wa.gov.au

🕐 Daily 9:30–5

PICA:

☎ (08) 9228 6300; www.pica.org.au

🕐 Tue–Sun 11–6 (Fri till 9)

More to see in Western Australia

ALBANY

Now a scenic holiday resort, Albany was Western Australia's first settlement. Founded three years before Perth, the town developed into a port and whaling centre. The old whaling station is now the fascinating Whale World museum, and there is whale watching here from August to October. The town contains the 1850s Residency and Old Gaol, both now museums. The coastline and beaches are spectacular, as is the rugged mountain country of Stirling Range National Park, which lies 100km (62 miles) inland.

www.albanytourist.com.au

🚻 14K 🚌 From Perth 🛈 Albany Visitor Centre ✉ Old Railway Station, Proudlove Parade ☎ (08) 9841 9290 🕙 Daily 9–5

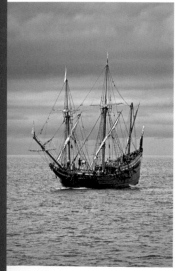

FREMANTLE

Perth's seaport is reached by train or a short boat trip down the Swan River. Fremantle's harbourside location, delightful old buildings and quaint streets make it irresistible. Don't miss the informative Western Australian Maritime Museum, the Fremantle Arts Centre, the markets, the historic Round House and Fremantle Prison.

www.fremantle.org.au

🚻 13J 🚌 or 🚆 Fremantle 🛈 Fremantle Tourist Bureau ✉ Town Hall, Kings Square ☎ (08) 9431 7878 🕙 Mon–Fri 9–5, Sat 10–3, Sun 11:30–2

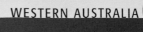

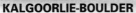

KALGOORLIE-BOULDER

Prospectors flocked to this barren Outback region, 600km (372 miles) east of Perth, when rich gold deposits were discovered near Kalgoorlie in 1893. The area still produces nickel and gold. The city of Kalgoorlie and its smaller neighbour, Boulder, contain fine old buildings, the Australian Prospectors and Miners Hall of Fame, at the Hannans North Mine complex, and a Royal Flying Doctor base. The well-preserved ghost town of Coolgardie is also worth a visit.

www.kalgoorlietourism.com

⊞ 15J 🚆 *Prospector* from Perth ✈ Kalgoorlie

🛈 Kalgoorlie Goldfields Visitor Centre ✉ Hannan Town Hall, corner Hannan and Wilson streets, Kalgoorlie ☎ (08) 9021 1966 🕐 Mon–Fri 8:30–5, Sat–Sun 9–5. Closed 25 Dec

THE KIMBERLEY

Best places to see, ➤ 48–49.

177

MARGARET RIVER

Some of Australia's best wines are produced around this picturesque town, 280km (174 miles) south of Perth, in over 50 wineries, including the excellent Vasse Felix and Leeuwin Estate. You can sample the wines produced at many of them. The area has wonderful beaches, great surfing and bushwalking along the cliffs of nearby Leeuwin-Naturaliste National Park. The Margaret River township has galleries, craft shops and fine restaurants.

www.margaretriver.com

🚉 13J 🚌 From Perth
ℹ️ Margaret River Tourist Bureau ✉️ 100 Bussell Highway, Margaret River ☎️ (08) 9780 5911
🕐 Daily 9–5. Closed 25 Dec

NAMBUNG NATIONAL PARK AND THE PINNACLES

This coastal national park to the north of Perth bristles with thousands of limestone pillars and needles reaching up to 6m (19ft) in height. Early Dutch seafarers believed they had sighted a ruined city, but the Pinnacles are actually the eroded remnants of a former thick bed of limestone. The area has good beaches.

www.dec.wa.gov.au

🔟 13J 📧 Nambung National Park, via Cervantes ☎ (08) 9652 7700
🕐 Daily 🖐 Inexpensive 🚌 None

PEMBERTON

A visit to the small town of Pemberton, at the heart of the southwest's 'Tall Timber Country', reveals a very different aspect of Western Australia. Giant 400-year-old hardwood trees – jarrah, karri and marri – tower 100m (330ft) above the dense undergrowth. Ride the Pemberton Tramway through the forests or walk the numerous trails.

www.pembertontourist.com.au

🔟 13K 🚌 From Perth
ℹ️ Pemberton Visitor Centre 📧 Brockman Street ☎ (08) 9776 1133
🕐 Daily 9–5. Closed 25 Dec

ROTTNEST ISLAND

This idyllic island lies just 90 minutes by ferry or 15 minutes by air from Perth. First discovered by Dutch seafarers in the 17th century and mistakenly named 'rat's nest' after the quokkas (small marsupials that still roam the island), Rottnest has almost 40km (25 miles) of extraordinarily white beaches, crystal-clear waters that are perfect for fishing, diving and snorkelling, and a relaxed, car-free atmosphere.

www.rottnest.wa.gov.au

➕ 13J 🚢 From Perth, Fremantle or Hillarys Boat Harbour ✋ Ferry fare: expensive (includes entrance fee to island)

ℹ Rottnest Island Visitor Centre ✉ Thomson Bay

☎ (08) 9372 9732 🕐 Daily 8:30–5

SHARK BAY

With islands and 1,500km (930 miles) of indented coastline, the World Heritage Site of Shark Bay, on the state's mid-north coast, is a marine wonderland. This vast inlet is

famous for Monkey Mia beach, where wild dolphins come close to the shore to be hand fed. Visit dazzlingly white Shell Beach and François Peron National Park, and see Hamelin Pool's stromatolites, some of the world's oldest living organisms.

www.sharkbay.org

➕ 1E ✋ Inexpensive

🚌 From Perth ℹ Shark Bay Tourist Bureau ✉ 89 Knight Terrace, Denham ☎ (08) 9948 1208 🕐 Daily 9–5

WAVE ROCK

This stunning rock formation is one of Western Australia's strangest natural wonders. Wave Rock is a 14m-high (46ft) granite wall, more than 100m (330ft) long, which has been eroded over almost 3,000 million years into the shape of a breaking wave. Other curious (and curiously named) formations in the area include the Breakers and the Hippo's Yawn, and you can also look at Aboriginal hand paintings at Mulkas Cave.

www.waverock.com.au

🚩 14J 🎟️ Inexpensive 🚌 From Perth to Hyden

🛈 Hyden Tourist Centre ✉️ 20 Marshall Street ☎️ (08) 9880 5182

🕐 Daily 9–5

a drive south of Perth

Taking in beautiful coastal scenery, this drive can just about be accomplished in a day – or you might want to stay overnight to fully appreciate the area.

Leave Perth via the Stirling Highway, then follow Cockburn Road and Patterson Road to Rockingham.

Make a brief stop at Rockingham, an attractive seaside resort offering excellent beaches and the chance to see fairy penguins at Penguin Island (Mar–Dec).

Continue south on the Mandurah Road.

Located on the coast at the mouth of idyllic Peel Inlet, Mandurah is the perfect spot for swimming, fishing and boating. There are boat cruises and opportunities to swim with dolphins (Nov–Jan).

Continue south on the Old Coast Road.

Yalgorup National Park offers a peaceful environment of swamps, lakes, dunes and woodland. Birdwatchers should look out for some of the 100 or so species of waterbird that frequent the area.

Continue south.

The popular seaside resort of Bunbury has good beaches and a harbour, and you might well see dolphins at Koombana Beach, where the Dolphin Discovery Centre is located. You can drive further south to see the tall 400-year-old trees of the Tuart Forest National Park. If you wish to stay in the area overnight, continue to Busselton and Margaret River (➤ 178).

Head back towards Perth on the fast South Western Highway.

Returning to Perth, stop at the historic town of Armadale (History House Museum), 30km (18 miles) from the city, the Araluen Botanic Park at Roleystone, and Cohunu Koala Park at Gosnells.

Continue on to Perth.

Distance 360km (224 miles) **Time** A full day at least
Start/end point Central Perth ✚ 13J
Lunch Benesse Cafe ($) ✉ 83 Victoria Street, Bunbury
☎ (08) 9791 4030

HOTELS

PERTH
Riverview on Mount Street ($$)
Situated close to the city centre and Kings Park, this hotel consists of self-contained studio apartments.
✉ 42 Mount Street ☎ (08) 9321 8963; www.riverviewperth.com.au
🚌 Central Area Transit bus

KALGOORLIE-BOULDER
All Seasons Plaza Hotel Kalgoorlie ($$)
This centrally located 100-room hotel has a pool, bar and restaurant on site.
✉ 45 Egan Street ☎ (08) 9021 4544; www.accorhotels.com.au 🚌 None

THE KIMBERLEY
El Questro Wilderness Park ($–$$$)
This vast cattle station provides everything from campsites and bungalows to luxurious rooms.
✉ Gibb River Road, via Kununurra ☎ 1300 134 044; www.elquestro.com.au
🚌 Transfer from Kununurra

MARGARET RIVER
Cape Lodge ($$$)
An award-winning lodge with colonial furniture, airy rooms and a rural atmosphere.
✉ Caves Road, Yallingup ☎ (08) 9755 6311; www.capelodge.com.au
🕐 Apr–Oct 🚌 None

RESTAURANTS

PERTH
Dusit Thai ($$)
Perth's Northbridge is full of good restaurants, including this established Thai eatery.
✉ 249 James Street, Northbridge ☎ (08) 9328 7647; www.dusitthai.com.au
🕐 Lunch Thu–Fri, dinner Tue–Sun 🚌 Central Area Transit bus

Fraser's ($$–$$$)
See page 61.

The Loose Box ($$$)
A half-hour drive from the city, this is arguably Western Australia's best restaurant with classic French cuisine.
✉ 6825 Great Eastern Highway, Mundaring ☎ (08) 9295 1787; www.loosebox.com 🕐 Lunch Sun, dinner Wed–Sat 🚐 None

ALBANY
Ristorante Leonardo's ($$)
Serving pastas and Italian steak, vegetarian and seafood dishes, this is one of Albany's most popular restaurants.
✉ 166 Stirling Terrace ☎ (08) 9841 1732 🕐 Dinner Tue–Sat 🚐 None

BUNBURY
Vat 2 ($–$$)
Vat 2 has a simple menu in stylish surrounds on the waterfront.
✉ 2 Jetty Road ☎ (08) 9791 8833 🕐 Lunch and dinner 🚐 None

FREMANTLE
Little Creatures ($–$$)
Located in one of WA's most distinguished beer breweries.
✉ 40 Mews Road ☎ (08) 9430 5155 🕐 Lunch and dinner daily 🚢 or 🚐 From Perth

The Red Herring ($$)
Classy Modern Australian restaurant, with excellent seafood.
✉ 26 Riverside Road, East Fremantle ☎ (08) 9339 1611; www.redherring.com.au 🕐 Lunch and dinner daily 🚂 Fremantle

KALGOORLIE-BOULDER
Judds Restaurant ($$)
Pub restaurant overlooking Kalgoorlie's main street. The speciality is wood-fired pizza.
✉ The Kalgoorlie Hotel, 319 Hannan Street ☎ (08) 9021 3046 🕐 Lunch and dinner daily 🚐 None

MARGARET RIVER
Leeuwin Estate Winery Restaurant ($$)
With an emphasis on fresh local produce, this elegant but casual restaurant offers Modern Australian dishes.

✉ Stevens Road ☎ (08) 9759 0000; www.leeuwinestate.com.au
🕐 Lunch daily, dinner Sat 🚌 None

SHOPPING

AUSTRALIANA AND ABORIGINAL ART
London Court
Tudor-style arcade offering Australiana souvenirs, gifts and shops.

✉ Between Hay Street Mall and St George's Terrace, Perth
☎ (08) 9261 6666; www.londoncourt.com.au 🚌 Central Area Transit bus

Creative Native
One of Perth's best Aboriginal art centres.

✉ Shop 58, Forrest Chase, Forrest Place, Perth ☎ (08) 9221 5800;
www.creativenative.com.au 🚉 Perth Station

SHOPPING CENTRE
Forrest Chase Shopping Plaza
This large, modern shopping centre is one of the best places to shop in Perth.

✉ Murray Street, between Forrest Place and Barrack Street, Perth
☎ (08) 9322 9111 🚉 Perth Station

ENTERTAINMENT

His Majesty's Theatre
This charming venue is the home of theatre and opera in Perth.

✉ 825 Hay Street, Perth ☎ (08) 9265 0900; www.hismajestystheatre.com.au
🚌 Central Area Transit bus

Margeaux's
Classy nightclub in one of Perth's best hotels, with bar and disco.

✉ Parmelia Hilton, 14 Mill Street, Perth ☎ (08) 9215 2000 🕐 Daily
🚌 Central Area Transit bus

Sight Locator Index

This index relates to the maps on the covers. We have given map references to the main sights of interest in the book. Grid references in italics indicate sights featured on the town plan. Some sights within towns may not be plotted on the maps.

Adelaide **20K**
Adelaide Hills **20K**
Albany **14K**
Alice Springs **7E**
Australian Museum
  Sydney 4f
Ballarat **21K**
Barossa Valley **20K**
Blue Mountains **23J**
Brisbane **24H**
Broken Hill **20J**
Byron Bay **24H**
Cairns and District **10C**
Canberra and the ACT **23K**
Carnarvon Gorge National Park **11E**
Charters Towers **10D**
Coffs Harbour **24H**
Dandenong Ranges **22K**
Darling Harbour *Sydney 2f*
Darwin **6B**
Flinders Ranges National Park **20J**
Fraser Island **12E**
Fremantle **13J**
Freycinet Peninsula **22M**
Gold Coast **24H**
Great Barrier Reef **11C**
Great Ocean Road **21L**
Hobart **22M**
Hunter Valley **23J**
Kakadu National Park **7B**
Kalgoorlie-Boulder **15J**
Kangaroo Island **19K**
Katherine **6B**
Kiama **23K**
The Kimberley **5C**
Lamington National Park **24H**
Launceston **22L**
Longreach **10E**
Lord Howe Island **24J (off map)**

Margaret River **13J**
Melbourne **21K**
The Midlands **22M**
Myall Lakes National Park **23J**
Nambung National Park and the
  Pinnacles **13J**
Nitmiluk National Park **6B**
Pemberton **13K**
Perth **13J**
Phillip Island **21L**
Port Arthur and the Tasman Peninsula
  22M
Powerhouse Museum *Sydney 2g*
The Rocks *Sydney 3b*
Rottnest Island **13J**
Shark Bay **1E**
Snowy Mountains **22K**
Southern Highlands **23K**
Strahan **21M**
Sunshine Coast **12E**
Sydney **23J**
Sydney Harbour Bridge *Sydney 3a*
Sydney Harbour and Sydney Opera
  House *Sydney 4a*
Sydney Tower *Sydney 3e*
Taronga Zoo *Sydney 3a (off map)*
Tasmania's World Heritage Area **22L**
  and 22M
Tiwi Islands **6B**
Townsville **10D**
Uluru-Kata Tjuta National Park **6E**
Watarrka National Park **6E**
Wave Rock **14J**
Wilsons Promontory National Park
  22L
Whitsunday Islands **11D**

187

Index

Acknowledgements

The Automobile Association would like to thank the following photographers, companies and picture libraries for their assistance in the preparation of this book.

Abbreviations for picture credits – (t) top; (b) bottom; (c) centre; (l) left; (r) right; (AA) AA World Travel Library; Aust: Australian; NP: National Park; SA: South Australia; WA: Western Australia; NT: Northern Territory; Qld: Queensland; Vic: Victoria; NT: Northern Territory; ATC: Australian Tourist Commission; WATC: Western Australia Tourist Commission; SATC: South Australia Tourist Commission

4l Sydney, AA/S Day; **4c** Milsons Point, Sydney, AA/M Langford; **4r** Great Barrier Reef, ATC; **5l** Great Ocean Rd, Vic, AA/B Bachman; **5r** Walkers nr Cradle Mtn, ATC; **6/7** Sydney, AA/S Day; **8/9** Finke Gorge NP, AA/A Baker, **10/11t** Surfers Paradise, AA/A Belcher; **10c** Acacias, AA/A Baker; **10bl** Sydney Harbour, AA/S Day; **10br** Merino sheep, AA/A Baker; **11c** Sydney, AA/S Day; **11b** Sam Lovell, AA/S Watkins; **12** Fish, AA/P Kenward; **12bl** Aboriginal tour, NT, AA/S Watkins; **12/3b** Restaurant, AA/B Bachman; **13t** Menu, AA/L K Stow; **13b** Queen Victoria Market, Melbourne, AA/B Bachman; **14t** Wine, AA/M Langford; **14b** Vineyard, Yarra Valley, Vic, Ern Mainka/Alamy; **15** Café, AA/M Langford; **16t** Sydney Opera House, AA/P Kenward; **16b** Bondi beach, AA/M Langford; **17** Ferry, Circular Quay, AA/M Langford, **18t** Lizard Island, Great Barrier Reef, Qld, Tourism Queensland; **18c** Koala, AA/A Belcher; **18/9** Ayers Rock, AA/A Baker; **19t** Koalas, AA/M Moody; **19b** Trekking, AA/M Cawood; **20/1** Milsons Point, AA/ M Langford; **24** National Tennis Centre, Melbourne, AA/ B Bachman; **25** Fringe Festival, Melbourne, AA/B Bachman; **28** The Ghan train, AA/ M Langford; **29** Road sign, AA /M Langford; **34/5** Great Barrier Reef, Aust TC; **36** Canyoning, AA/S Richmond; **36/7** Blue Mtns, AA/P Kenward; **38/9t** Kuranda, AA/A Belcher; **38/9b** Port Douglas, AA/A Belcher; **39** (inset) Birdworld, Kuranda, AA/A Belcher; **40** Wet 'n' Wild Water World, AA/A Belcher; **40/1** Warner Brothers Movie World, AA/A Belcher; **41tr** Narrow Neck, Gold Coast, Qld, Tourism Queensland; **42** Great Barrier Reef, AA/A Baker; **42/3** Divers, AA/A Baker; **43** Townsville, AA/A Belcher; **44/5t** Great Ocean Rd, AA/B Bachman; **44/5b** Great Ocean Rd, Aust TC/David Simmons; **46** Kakadu NP, AA/S Watkins; **46/7t** Kakadu NP, AA/S Watkins; **46/7b** Nourlangie Rock, AA/S Watkins; **48** The Kimberley, ATC; **48/9** The Kimberley, AA/S Watkins; **50/1t** Sydney Opera House, AA/S Day; **50/1b** Sydney Harbour, AA/M Langford; **51** (inset) Sydney Opera House, ATC; **52/3** Cradle Mtn, AA/S Richmond; **53t** Mt Ossa, AA/S Richmond; **54/5** Ayers Rock, AA/S Richmond; **56/7** Great Ocean Rd, AA/B Bachman; **58t** Kangaroo, AA/P Kenward; **58b** Diver, Ningaloo Marine Park, Tourism Western Australia; **59** Trekking, Tasmania, AA/S Richmond; **60** Doyle's on the Beach, AA/P Kenward; **62/3** Cape Otway, Aust TC; **64/5** Mt Coot-tha, AA/A Belcher; **66/7t** Tiwi Islands, AA/S Watkins; **66/7b** AA/B Bachman; **68/9** Hotel, AA/B Bachman; **70/1** Street performer, AA/B Bachman; **72** The Rocks Market, AA/M Langford; **74/5** Sydney Harbour, AA/S Day; **75** Iron railings, AA/S Day; **76/7** The Rocks Market, AA/S Day; **78/9** Walkers nr Cradle Mtn, Aust TC; **81** Hunter Valley, AA/S Day; **82/3t** Aust Museum AA/S Day; **82/3b** Darling Harbour, AA/S Day; **84** The Rocks, AA/M Langford; **84/5** The Rocks, AA/M Langford; **85** Sydney Harbour Bridge, AA/P Kenward; **86** Sydney Tower, AA/P Kenward; **87** Taronga Zoo, AA/S Day; **88** National Botanic Gardens, AA/A Baker; **88/9** Aust War Memorial, AA/P Kenward; **90/1** Parliament House, AA/P Kenward; **91** Parliament House, AA/A Baker; **92/3** Byron Bay Lighthouse, Aust TC; **94** Blue Mtns, AA/P Kenward; **96t** Hunter Valley, AA/S Day; **96b** Hunter Valley, AA/S Day; **97** Kangaroo Valley, AA/P Kenward; **98/9** Mt Kosciuszko, AA/S Richmond; **99l** Moss Vale, AA/P Kenward; **99r** Morton NP, AA/P Kenward; **105** Noosa, AA/A Belcher; **107** Brisbane Botanic Gardens, AA/A Belcher; **108** Mt Coot-tha, AA/A Belcher; **108/9** South Bank, AA/A Belcher; **110/11** Charters Towers, AA/A Belcher; **111** Charters Towers, AA/A Belcher; **112** Fraser Island, AA/A Belcher; **112/3** Fraser Island, AA/A Belcher; **113** Lamington NP, AA/A Belcher; **114** Noosa, AA/A Belcher; **114/5** Noosa Heads, AA/A Belcher; **115** Pelican, AA/A Belcher; **116/7t** Townsville, AA/A Belcher; **116/7b** Townsville, AA/A Belcher; **117** Whitsunday Islands, AA/ L K Stow; **118** Daintree, AA/A Belcher; **119** Cape Tribulation, AA/A Belcher; **123** Federation Square, Melbourne, AA/B Bachman; **125** The Edge, Eureka Skydeck; **126/7** Melbourne Cricket Ground, Peter Dunphy/Visions of Victoria; **128/9** St Kilda, AA/B Bachman; **129t** St Kilda, AA/B Bachman; **129b** St Kilda, AA/B Bachman; **130/1** Yarra River, AA/B Bachman; **131** Royal Botanic Gardens, AA/B Bachman; **132/3** Ballarat, AA/B Bachman; **132** Ballarat, AA/B Bachman; **133t** Dandenong Ranges, AA/B Bachman; **133b** Puffing Billy, AA/B Bachman; **134/5** Phillip Island, AA/B Bachman; **136** Hobart, AA/A Baker; **136/7** Hobart, AA/A Baker; **138/9** Freycinet NP, AA/N Rains; **140** Launceston, AA/A Baker; **140/1** Cataract Gorge, AA/A Baker; **142** Penitentiary, Port Arthur Historic Site, Tasmania, Fabian Gonzales Editorial/Alamy; **147** Flinders Ranges NP, AA/M Cawood; **148/9** Art Gallery of SA **149** Art Gallery of SA **150** Glenelg City, Adelaide,SATC; **152** Adelaide Botanic Garden, SATC/Milton Wordley; **154** National Motor Museum, Birdwood, SATC/Adelaide Hills Tourism/Adam Bruzzone; **154/5** Adelaide Hills, SATC/Adam Bruzzone; **155** Grant Burge Filsell Vineyard, Barossa, Grant Burge Wines Pty Ltd; **156** Flinders Ranges NP, AA/M Cawood; **156/7** Flinders Ranges NP, AA/M Cawood; **157** Kangaroo Island, SA Tourist Board; **159t** The Ghan, Darwin Railway Station, Tourism NT/David Silva; **158/9b** Stokes Hill Wharf, Darwin, Look Die Bildagentur der Fotografen GmbH/Alamy; **160/1t** George Brown Darwin Botanic Gardens, Tourism NT; **160/1b** Mindil Beach, Tourism NT/Barry Skipsey; **162** Alice Springs, AA/S Richmond; **162/3** Alice Springs, AA/S Richmond; **163** Tiwi dancers, AA/S Watkins; **164/5** Kings Canyon, AA/S Richmond; **165** Kings Canyon, AA/ S Richmond; **166/7** Tjaynera Falls, AA/S Watkins; **167** Litchfield NP, AA/S Watkins; **171** The Kimberley, AA/S Watkins; **172/3t** Swan Bells viewing platform, AA/ M Langford; **172/3b** Perth, AA/ M Langford; **174/5** Kings Park, AA/M Langford; **176** Fremantle, AA/ M Langford; **176/7** Kalgoorlie, AA/A Baker; **178t** Margaret River, AA/M Langford; **178b** Margaret River, AA/M Langford; **179** The Pinnacles, AA/A Baker; **180** Shell Beach, AA/A Baker; **180/1** Wave Rock, WA Tourism; **182/3** Bunbury, WATC.

Every effort has been made to trace the copyright holders, and we apologise in advance for any accidental errors. We would be happy to apply any corrections to following editions of this publication.